SAVING DEMOCRACY!

SAVING DEMOCRACY!

How Good Management Could Trump Ideological Bickering

BILL GREENE

Illustrations by Bruce Greene

ISBN-13: 9781523417049
ISBN-10: 1523417048
Library of Congress Control Number: 2016901027
CreateSpace Independent Publishing Platform
North Charleston, South Carolina

TABLE OF CONTENTS

INTRODUCTION

The upcoming 2016 election is giving Americans one more chance to reverse the downward slide in our nation's well-being. I remain, like Charlie Brown, ever-optimistic. After all, voters have come to recognize, whether they are liberal or conservative, young or old, that too many of our representatives in Washington are either incompetent or corrupt, or both! A majority of American men and women have lost confidence in our elected leadership, *which well they should.*

In the following pages we will outline what our major problems are and what we must do to fix America's broken government. Such a goal may sound presumptuous, but understand that the best solutions often come from ordinary men and women, like you and me, using common sense, unburdened by the abstract notions of all the "experts." Saving America can be quite simple if we just concentrate on the important issues and stop all the ideological bickering.

Elections and government affairs have fascinated me ever since our family woke up on November 3, 1948 and heard that Harry Truman had somehow come from behind and won the presidency. We had gone to bed the night before quite dismayed by the apparent victory of Tom Dewey, the Republican governor of New York. But the morning news brought us fresh hope and delight—Harry Truman had come from behind to win a second term as the president of the United States.

In those days, we were all "died-in-the-wool" Democrats because Franklin Roosevelt had shown everyone in the world that he would take care of the common people—and we were as common as you can get! My brother and I had a working single mom, an absent and uncaring father, and we lived on the wrong side of the tracks. My political leanings moved to the right in later years, but there is little doubt that Harry Truman turned out to be one of our great presidents. Truman was followed by General Dwight Eisenhower, "Ike," our president from 1952-1960. Those were the days when America enjoyed boom times, peace and prosperity, and an honest and effective government.

At the time that Ike was elected, I was working on a research grant to evaluate his appointments to fill the top posts in our government. I assumed at that time that having competent and experienced managers running the nation was the norm and Ike's appointments did not disappoint. Two of his top picks had the same name, Charles Wilson, so they became known as "Electric Charlie" and "Engine Charlie," because one had been CEO at General Electric and the other at General Motors. Running those giant organizations, after working their way up for years to the top, ensured Ike that he would be dealing with very capable individuals who would run their departments in an accomplished manner. And, of course, Ike had just come off a storied career himself, having led the Allied war effort and the massive invasions that had crushed Hitler's horrid Nazi regime.

The resulting Eisenhower administration gave America one of its best managed governments ever and still managed to outlaw school segregation, strengthen social security, end the Korean War, reduce racial discrimination, and bring the spread of Soviet communism to a halt. It was not hard to become an admirer of Ike because he proved to be a capable chief executive with a big heart. And he stood tall; all the world leaders respected our country and our president! We didn't have to apologize to anyone!

In the many years since that time I have worked in hundreds of organizations as an outside business advisor, a financial auditor, and as a consultant on the effectiveness of their operational structure. In the process, I have come to recognize and appreciate well-run outfits that are both supportive of their people and financially sound.

It is ironic that today, fifty years after Eisenhower's well-run administration, America's biggest organization, the federal bureaucracy, is neither well managed nor honestly led, and that some leading politicians are deeply distrusted because of their long record of lies, cover-ups, and hypocrisy. It seems that nowadays the more crooked a politician is, the more sycophants will hang on their coattails and tell us how honest they are! I have been witness to the last thirteen presidents and I can assure you that times have changed, and not for the better—most of our recent leaders have proven to be dishonest or bad administrators, or both— and they are killing America!

Anyone familiar with America's thousands of corporations can understand that such illustrious names as Kellogg, 3M, Merck, General Motors, Johnson & Johnson, and Colgate have supplied the jobs and quality products that have made Americans prosperous and secure. They have each operated successfully for about a hundred years and are active in hundreds of foreign nations where they get along with those people and governments considerably better than our State Department. But that's the "private sector." Each of those companies is in A+ financial shape, pays large amounts of taxes to the government, earns a normal return on their invested capital, supplies an essential product to the public, competes successfully with a number of equally well-run competitors, employs thousands of workers, and pays about a 3 percent dividend to the millions of owners who saved some money and invested in their stock. What's not to like about all that?

There is a reason that America's public sector has not matched the good performance of a Johnson & Johnson over the last century: We have been electing inexperienced amateurs to manage our huge government and its agencies. They have passed millions of laws and regulations and created thousands of government departments and programs. They have sympathized with the new academic and radical liberal elite that is attacking America. Many have denigrated our religions, business, patriotism, marriage, and self-reliance. They have produced no products and created no jobs except for an expanding government workforce, but they have criticized the hell out of everything good in America.

Instead of managing our country, our politicians have continually meddled in foreign affairs, giving away billions of dollars and taking picture ops of their endless and unsuccessful negotiations to create "world peace." And when it comes to domestic affairs, they seem to concentrate on "changing" America rather than managing the government we have. America is one of the best nations that ever existed; we don't elect leaders to change it—we just need them to run the country honestly and efficiently. We need political leaders who will fix America, not keep destroying it.

Readers should be aware that the following pages will challenge many of their notions and ask them to reconsider the politically correct mantras that are crippling our thinking. For starters, it should be self-evident that people are very different from one another in countless ways. Those differences result in the fact that some people are worse, or better, than others. God reputedly loves us all, but when it comes to being part of a community, some people contribute to the society's well being, while others detract or are a burden on the community. Now, most everyone agrees that each individual deserves equal rights and respect under the laws of God and nations, but there is no denying that successful nations are built and maintained by those who contribute in a positive way and are burdened by those who don't.

Just as with people, the world's cultures, governments, and religions vary, and wherever there are differences, you will find differences in quality. You can respect and sympathize with the culture of Uganda, the government of North Korea, and the religion of Saudi Arabia, but it is totally irrational to consider them the equals of what one sees in Sweden, England, or Japan. Today's curious notions about multiculturalism, moral relativism, and the love of "diversity" are hurting our ability to make decisions and set policies—and the foolishness behind these false notions is analyzed in the chapters that follow.

A different odd notion we will critique, one that seriously hurts our people and finances, is the notion that America has to be the policeman and pastor to the world. Virtually every candidate for office wants our State Department and military forces to keep meddling abroad in other peoples' business. In 1953, when Eisenhower first took office he defined America's course in foreign affairs: "Any nation's right to form a government and an economic system of its own choosing is inalienable. Any nation's attempt to dictate to other nations their form of government is indefensible." He thereby reaffirmed George Washington's words in his Farewell Address of over a century and a half before when we were warned "to avoid foreign entanglements."

Unfortunately, our last three presidents have abandoned that wisdom and have been busy bombing and invading around the world trying to impose our ideas on others. That's not good leadership. When I was at the Hague Academy of International Law, we knew that a fundamental precept of international law, one that has been recognized for centuries, is that a nation that invades others is an aggressor and stands in clear violation of the law of nations.

And it must be equally true that using drones and planes to target and execute foreign nationals in their homeland is both immoral and a violation of law.

In 1961, at the end of his two terms in office, Ike advised us about the future: To protect our peaceful existence we were told to maintain the mightiest armed forces in the world so no one would attack us, but guard against excess influence by the military-industrial complex that could endanger our liberty. It seems incomprehensible that recent presidents have ignored that warning, meddled in other nations' affairs, sent our soldiers to die in fruitless wars, and created a coercive surveillance state that threatens to invade our lives and freedom. Even more incredible, they added a trillion dollars to our national debt to pay for those failed foreign adventures.

"Every gun that is made," Ike declared, "every warship launched, every rocket fired signifies in the final sense, a theft from those who hunger and are not fed, those who are cold and not clothed...This is not a way of life at all...Under the cloud of threatening war, it is humanity hanging from a cross of iron."[1] Today, those words remain more true than ever. Democrats and Republicans alike point at the Islamic State and want war, but the Islamic State has no air force, no navy, next to no tanks or artillery.[2] It has no path to invading America except through our porous borders. As FDR said, "We have nothing to fear but fear itself." Perhaps we should stay out of foreign conflicts and just concentrate on protecting our borders and homes.

It is my hope that every reader will become aware of why we must restore "justice" as a fundamental foundation of American culture. Government actions are increasingly being designed to help particular segments of the nation. Now, for many of you, "helping" may sound good, but when parceled out to selected groups, it becomes *preferential politics*, which is, in essence, unfair to everyone not included. For example, the 10 percent ethanol mandate helps corn growers but hurts everyone else; ethnic quotas help one group while creating an injustice for others; and the "carried interest" tax loophole helps Wall Street traders but hurts everyone else. Our leaders are playing with us, setting one group against another, handing out freebies for votes. That's how you train a dog! But there's no justice in it for those of us not being thrown a bone!

We need a return to fairness, where every child will be assured of equal opportunity, and there will truly be *liberty and justice for all*. This will require a persistent War on Corruption and the creation of a level playing field for everyone. America's biggest enemy is not external, like ISIS or China, but right here at home—from the corruption and inexperience of our government officials.

Today's national leadership may have failed to manage the country well, but they have been excellent "managers" of our peoples' minds. They have, over the last few decades, managed to turn many people's minds against the successful organizations that can claim credit for our country's safety and prosperity—namely our religious, military, and business enterprises. And yet, those are the organizations, run by millions of Americans, that built our success. No other nation can claim to be home to a fraction of such great and well managed organizations.

In contrast, our elected leaders appoint their partisan financial supporters and political hacks to run the major departments of government. None of them have seemed to care about the waste, inefficiency, and corruption that is endemic throughout most of the federal government. It is well known that professional politicians have virtually no management or business experience, so it is understandable that they have no idea how to run anything or fix anything. But shouldn't they have at least tried somewhere during the last few decades?

Governors do represent an exception; once elected, they have a chance to learn on the job and may *become* competent managers. Ohio's governor, John Kasich, is an example of an honest and successful governor who has done a good job managing the state of Ohio and developing programs that have helped the people and the economy under his watch. However, he has not captured the voters' attention in the primary contests to date. Perhaps a candidate has to not only display ability but also the determination to get things done. Businessman Donald Trump has won a huge following because he has that "get-er done!" personality and even the evangelicals seem to prefer that over the usual promises and endless policy debates. The Trump supporters may be right in wanting a person of action because the mainstream politicians want no change in their cozy fiefdoms. It will take something like a bull-in-a-china-shop to disrupt their power and accomplish the changes we must have to save America.

Successful candidates for office have usually won by convincing voters that they are passionate about their ideas to make things better. The voters have usually been attracted more by the promises and so-called "expertise" of a candidate than by any evidence of honesty or management ability. Unfortunately, the candidates are not concerned with the millions of recipients in the Social Security system that were born before 1901 (apparently the computers are not equipped with a delete button). They are not concerned that the State Department cannot locate the hundreds of thousands of visitors who have overstayed their visa periods. Let's face it—the candidates just want to get elected, and re-elected. Honest intentions are notably missing.

The result is that most officials elected to the executive or legislative branches do not manage or supervise anything.

Instead, they spend their time arguing over political topics, renaming post offices, voting wasteful "pork" to their constituents, campaigning, fund raising for the next election, and living the good life in Washington. And the president is often the worst offender.

What we need is for our elected representatives to spend less time on the non-essential issues, such as the need for transgender bathroom facilities, and instead, simplify the government and the tax code, stop giving money to foreign governments that hate us, stop appointing Wall Street bankers to run the Treasury Department, and bring our troops safely home. Their job should be easy—just set aside the divisive ideologies, restore honesty and sound management to the government, and stop the bickering.

My essays here are heartfelt because they come from a great appreciation of the opportunities I have had in life and the hope that such blessings can continue to be extended and benefit a larger number of Americans. Our goal must be to always remain rational and fight for justice and a sound resurrection of America's fundamental strengths. Ben Carson concluded his recent book with these words: "I pray that with God's blessings our past will be but a stepping stone to a bright future and that our best days will truly lie ahead of us—a beautiful new beginning."[3] We can all say "Amen" to that, but it will definitely require a *new* beginning!

PART I
ARE ALL PEOPLE AND
GOVERNMENTS EQUAL?

Chapter 1

ARE DEMOCRACIES REALLY ALL THAT GREAT?

It is obvious to most people that a society that has offered personal liberty and a chance to participate in four hundred years of unprecedented growth and prosperity, fully deserves to be praised as a very exceptional nation. The Declaration of Independence rings out with the earliest Americans' stirring demand for liberty and all the benefits it has conferred. That inspiring guarantee of liberty is what has always made democracies the preferred choice of responsible men and women.

However, America was built by prior generations— the people of fifty years ago and a hundred years ago, and two hundred years ago. Our current leaders are merely living off the momentum of past Americans and there are signs that, like all democracies in history, we may not be able to retain our greatness much longer. But note that, if we do falter, our failure will not occur because of what is decided over abortion rights, gun control, climate change, legalized drugs, women's rights, or any of those social issues. None of those issues will make or break America. Instead, the failure will be caused by the almost fanatical ideological arguments expended over those hot button issues; the feverish passion, fanned and inflamed by political demagogues, all of which diverts us from what really matters.

Our children used to be taught Emma Lazarus's inspiring message engraved on The Statue of Liberty, a message that symbolizes the hopes and dreams of all mankind:

"Give me your tired, your poor,
Your huddled masses yearning to breathe free,
The wretched refuse of your teeming shore.
Send these, the homeless, tempest-tossed, to me:
I lift my lamp beside the golden door."

America's children knew these words to be true because they were the children or grandchildren of immigrants themselves. They had heard first hand of the evils their parents and ancestors had left behind, and how thankful they were to be in America. People around the world heard of the great new nation in the New World. For almost 400 years there has been a continuous flood of these "tempest-tossed" individuals pouring into America. They come from all over, very few leave, and today they flood in illegally—anyway they can manage, to partake of the American bounty of freedom and plenty.

The good side of all that is that America has truly been an exceptional democracy, and, for the last one hundred years, America has been the defender of the free world. The unfortunate side of all that, however, is that democracies have throughout history proven to be temporary forms of government. Historical averages suggest that 250 years is when democracies start to falter, decline, and fall into the dustbin of history. If that's the case, our time is up in nine years, in 2025, if you start counting from our 1775 Declaration of Independence. That doesn't give us much time to act decisively and solve all the problems that are crippling America!

The recent debates between the Republican and Democratic candidates for the 2016 presidential election reveal America's weakness: the endless bickering about who said what and when on relatively unimportant issues only serve to obscure the real problems we face. We must put behind us such less critical issues as who was against gay rights before they were for it. A lesson of history is that democracies usually disappear from the world stage with a pathetic whimper, brought on by the same types of corruption and divisive ideological battles that we see going on today in Washington.

Instead of engaging in ideological arguments over gun show sales or in which trimester to outlaw abortions, the question before us today is how to prevent the seemingly unstoppable inner rot that invades vibrant growing democracies and brings them to their knees. If we are to avoid that miserable fate, we must find a way to strengthen and renew our people and the culture that they built. And it must be done by perfecting our country, not by tearing it down.

The politicians in Washington have responded to the growing critique of America by creating hundreds of new laws and programs to battle the existence of poverty, discrimination, and inequality. But they did nothing to curb corruption, and the "cures" they came up with to help the economy have too often done more harm than good. There is no denying the obvious truth that our elected representatives are flunking their job of managing the country. What is not known is just what the people will do to fix America. What is known is that there will be no beneficial change if we keep electing the same type of ineffective characters that hold office today.

History's 250 year rule is partly explained by the fact that it takes that long for a growing nation to accumulate a significant class of intellectuals and "experts." Ralph Waldo Emerson has been called "America's first intellectual," and he appeared *after* we had become a top world power and

250 years after the first Americans landed on our shores. A nation has to be very rich and successful to support a class of individuals who do nothing but offer opinions, and usually just second-hand opinions at that! Although the intellectual elite never participate in the original growth of a nation, such experts feel free to critique those who did and to promote new ideas that serve to undermine the culture that worked! Can you believe it?! These experts are telling our children that our history is evil, that we do not deserve to be so rich, so powerful, or the most respected nation in the world. Their idea of progress is to remove the names of Columbus, Washington, and Lincoln from our national holidays! Their idea of international leadership is to apologize to third-rate authoritarian countries.

Educators have even slipped their anti-America message into the classrooms. Our children are now "taught" how evil it was to drop an atomic bomb on Hiroshima, the fact that women had no voting rights in the original Constitution, that slavery continued until the Civil War, about internment camps for some minorities during World War II, the continuation of racial discrimination since the Civil War, the continued plague of hunger and poverty, the war on women, and so on. The virulent emphasis put on these attacks about past sins is unprecedented and unremitting. If enough people end up believing that we are second-rate, we will be. Our democracy is under siege!

The criticisms have ignored many of our real problems and instead concentrated on past failings that have been remedied. Instead of taking pride for ending such failings and acknowledging the fact that we have made constant reforms, the critiques have been extended into the regions of the absurd. How can we protect people from scalding coffee at McDonald's? How can we bail out those who didn't understand an adjustable rate mortgage? How do we protect people from getting high on drugs? And some even want laws limiting calories and soft drinks to prevent obesity! And all that nonsense takes place while the president is sending our young men and women to overseas battles where they get killed and crippled for no good reason and in places where we don't belong!

The question now before us is: What are the things that should be made better? The word "better" means many different things to different people. The current chasm that separates Americans into two broad groups is built around this conflict of vision.[4] There is one group who resist change and seek to protect the values and culture that created America. The other group want, in President Obama's words, to fundamentally transform America. Note that the latter group's desires are not about what *they* want to do, but rather about the things that they want *government* to do. All their plans involve governmental action, and it is mostly about re-distribution, taking from one group and giving to another. That is what politics and government action has come to; not to improve our governing institutions, not to maintain a fair workplace for all, not to encourage job creation, but to manipulate the prosperity we have and to swap favors for votes and money.

Think for a minute about that "manipulation" by our state, local, and federal governments. They have no money to do anything with except what they take from the workers and businesses—the productive private sector where everything in the nation that is of any value or use is made, served, and traded. Currently the governments take over one-third of everything produced. They use that

> "One of the key problems today is that politics is such a disgrace; good people don't go into government."
>
> ---Donald J. Trump

money to employ twenty-two million workers, one-sixth of the nation's workforce. The amounts have grown so large that America has morphed into a populist democracy– the type that spends itself to death. But, the spending by itself isn't the real problem. It's the fact that the spending comes from borrowed money that makes it so perilous. Differing ideologies will never break America, but corruption, deficits, and debt will do us in. You can argue forever about ideologies, but moral and financial bankruptcy have a time line.

The hypocrisy of the political establishment is that instead of improving our finances and institutions, they pander to special interest groups, set class against class, and hide their actions from the public. They say that they want to make life easier for the lower and middle classes, but they keep appointing the bankers to run the economy, creating speculative bubbles, then bailing out those on Wall Street who caused the crash

The elites in Washington lie to the voters, subsidize the bankers, steal from the public, and feather their own nests. Behind the scenes, some of our most well-known politicians take millions of dollars in "gifts" from foreign governments. Only the honest ones leave office without becoming multi-millionaires. Meanwhile, the Supreme Court does little to curb the corruption and the media distorts the news and covers the felons' tracks. And all the while, income inequality keeps getting worse, and the economy weaker.

Some ominous signs of the time are that there is a smaller percentage of working-age Americans actually working than ever before, illegitimate births have skyrocketed in just the last forty years, two-parent families are disappearing, the number of people receiving government aid keeps growing, while those working decline, the inner cities are becoming wastelands with crime, murders, violent gangs, truancy, drugs, and an exploding welfare load threatens everyone's economic future. Our foreign policy is in shambles with little respect from abroad, and declining trust from our former allies, government regulation and taxes are choking new businesses and the middle class, and schools are failing to teach half the students the rudiments of reading, writing, and arithmetic. These are the issues we must address and they should take precedence over the arguments about transgender bathroom facilities!

That's over a dozen major problems hurting the nation and I don't recall any of them being significant issues sixty years ago— they have all blossomed in the last fifty years! It is not a coincidence that that period was when government grew the most, did the most, and hurt the most. Aside from winning the Cold War, and making some reduction in discrimination against minorities, how many good things have happened at the national level during the last fifty years? And yet there are over a dozen major negative developments listed in the preceding paragraph, and we didn't even mention the deficits and the national debt!

The government and a few elites at the top, especially the major Wall Street financial firms and a few top Silicon Valley corporations, have actually gotten in bed together and are running the government for their mutual benefit, while promising the public that they will crack down on the top 1%. What is missed in all this is that "the top

1%" includes a variety of folks: No one complains about Hollywood entertainers and professional athletes earning tens or hundreds of millions of dollars. And, no one should complain about the business tycoons who created the internet, improved electronics, or developed better medicines and merchandising services, and thereby entered the top one percent! It is the financiers and speculators on Wall Street that brought on the 2008 crash who do not deserve being there– and they still are! Our president keeps appointing them!

The politicians' promises have been exposed as flagrantly dishonest by the fact that Wall Street bankers and speculators are still raking in more income than ever. That corrupt portion of the top one percent possess an increasing share of the nation's wealth, and the politicians are getting billions in contributions from them. Some politicians even get half a million dollars for a "speaking" fee! In return, top executives from Wall Street continue to run the treasury and justice departments! What we have is a repeat of the collapsing Roman Empire all over again.

The sad truth is that our beautiful democracy has grown too big, too opaque, too complex, and too overrun with special interest groups. Its "old-fashioned" culture is being undermined by a new love of diversity, moral relativism, and excess spending, regulation, and taxation. We are spinning out of control. Congress passes one thousand page bills into law that they haven't even read! The president signs the bills and issues executive orders to do whatever he and his supporters want. Instead of a democracy, we already have despots running the nation, by-passing the Constitution, and feathering their own nests. The two major political parties are locked in a stalemate. Our leaders meddle in foreign affairs ineffectively, sending our brave troops to die and be maimed in foreign wars that we can't win, don't understand, and don't even pursue with any consistency.

What has happened? Look at the history of all those past democracies and republics that have toppled from internal decay. We face nothing new. History is full of examples. Many wonderful praiseworthy republics have done well for a couple hundred years until they grew large and prosperous, overpopulated, overextended, and too complex for the voters to comprehend. It has happened a number of times; the pattern is clear. Free nations are a delicate breed.

The historical record proves that democracies are *temporary* forms of government. Rather than hide from that danger we must face it and act! We are whirling out of control. Neither the officials nor the public seem to have a clue how to fix it all. And many have no desire to even try! And yet, America is famous for having some of the best managers in the world. The problem seems to be that our most capable people don't seek political offices. And if one does, he or she is attacked by the Washington establishment, the media, and special interest groups.

Unfortunately, it makes no sense for successful executives to expose themselves to the vicious attacks from the public and the media that beset a politician—especially if that "combat" type of duty comes with a major pay-cut. A person would have to be very dedicated to improving the nation's fortunes or finding some illicit way to improve their own! That is why so many undesirables are attracted to politics— they either are ideologically driven to transform the culture, or they assume that they will earn a lot "on the side." That is a weakness of democracies—they require honest people with noble intentions. When a democracy's top offices are taken over by liars, cheats, and thieves, the government can no longer work for its people. And when those cheats are also incompetent, the government will probably work *against* the people's best interests.

Today's America, degraded by crony capitalism, where the politicians and a small elite are united in an effort to grab as much as they can, is no longer working. Income inequality has risen to unacceptable levels. The playing field is tilted against the working man. Neither the Republicans nor the Democrats show any interest in changing the status-quo. In America, with conditions so altered for the worse, the question is: Can democracy work here any longer, and if not, what can be done to save us?

Chapter 2

ARE WE REALLY ALL EQUAL??

It is safe to say that most people with an ounce of common sense would agree that people are not equal. You don't need a degree from a major university, or a position as an "expert" at some think tank, to know that everyone is unique and different from everyone else. We all know this truth and it is based on our first-hand interactions with fellow citizens: all men and women are created as unique individuals, unequal in many ways, with different characters, abilities, appearances, and personalities. That is why we must forget any idea of income equality—that would be a socialist myth, a fool's paradise, and a utopian dream.

But wait! That is not what Thomas Jefferson wrote in our Declaration of Independence. He wrote that "We hold these truths to be self-evident, that all men are created equal, that they are endowed by their Creator with certain unalienable rights, that among these are Life, Liberty, and the pursuit of happiness." However, a few weeks before Jefferson wrote all that, another Founding Father of America, George Mason, described our equality quite differently when he drafted the Virginia Bill of Rights. Mason wrote in that Virginia document that: "All men are by nature equally free and independent, and have certain inherent rights—namely, the enjoyment of life and liberty, with the means of acquiring and possessing property, and pursuing and obtaining happiness and safety."

"All men are born free and independent." James Mason

Mason's words, although less stirring than Jefferson's, are certainly more accurate. Mason carefully avoided any suggestion that people are equal. Instead he emphasized the responsibility of each individual to "pursue, acquire, and possess" whatever he or she wanted in life.

The intent in both of these historic documents was that all men should be free, should be treated fairly, with equal justice, and that they are equal in the sight of God, and have the right to equal opportunity in the pursuit of their personal goals and happiness. But Jefferson goes further than

Mason. Jefferson writes that "all men are created equal," while Mason merely writes that "all men are equally free and independent." There's a big difference between the two and it has led to some confusion in most people's minds about the nature of our equality.

To further complicate the matter, we will see in later sections of this book that Jefferson actually did believe in a "natural aristocracy" that included individuals of extra merit. This is not surprising because Jefferson was a great believer in self-improvement, and consciously conducted himself in accordance with numerous rules of behavior. It was that self-discipline that helped elevate him to the personal excellence he attained. Jefferson was very aware that different environments, the application of free will, and different levels of experience, could result in very different adults, with some people becoming more capable than others.

We know that the influence of the cultural environment, training, nutrition, and self-improvement all can help or hurt a child. But we also know, and Jefferson may not have known, that those formative forces have to start with and build on each individual's inherited biology. With all those forces acting on a variable set of genes, it is inevitable that each person develops into a unique character.

Some people find it convenient to gloss over that fact and assume that all persons are pretty much the same, and to then ignore the significance of the actual differences. That is why many people allow their generous disposition to overlook the differences in people. It may be kind and convenient to endorse diversity, to say that all people and cultures are equally good, but such thinking muddles some very important issues. In fact, people are different; and all the societies, religions, and governments around the world are different; and where there are differences, there are differences in quality.

The problem with worshipping diversity in and of itself is that such a blanket blessing blinds us to the reality of what is good and what is bad, what is right and what is wrong. If our youth are taught that the beliefs and attitudes within all cultures are equal, what do they have to model themselves after? And, why would one even bother to try and improve oneself? That kind of attitude can suck the ambition from a child.

Today's scientists who study the intricate workings of our bodies have made progress in explaining the biological nature of different personalities. Cloninger's model of personality separates three elements: novelty seeking, harm avoidance, and reward dependence. These traits in individuals can be traced to specific areas of the brain where individual differences make their bearers more or less impulsive, anxious, worried, or emotionally needy. It is that mix of all such inborn personality traits that influence a person throughout his or her life and makes people so fascinatingly interesting.

Another model, the five factor model, distinguishes between people that are gregarious, adventuresome, conscientious, cooperative, or emotionally unstable. Each trait has been traced to the operation of specific brain areas, primarily to the pre-frontal cortex, which is involved in planning and the voluntary control of behavior. These genetic forces play a meaningful role in defining who we are, how we behave, and how well we perform in our lives. It is such differences that make some people artists, mechanics, doctors, criminals, entrepreneurs, and generals; and those differences are also one of the causes of income inequality.

Teachers might like it if everyone were an A student; polite, obedient, and never missing a home-work assignment! But a nation of such individuals would never work well, never break barriers, nor advance with new ways of doing and thinking. If we were all the same, one form of education would work, any employment would be equally satisfying, and freedom would be largely irrelevant. (We are not "worker bees," even if it sometimes feels that way!) If we were duplicates of each other, what individual worth would there be in any one person? That would be a very unwanted form of equality!

Since it is clear that people differ so much, wouldn't it be helpful to find a better way to measure their talents? That way our schools might be able to figure out how to help them develop whatever skills they do have so they can grow into confident and happy adults. Currently our schools and colleges concentrate on the brightest; the rest are left to fend for themselves, and many do not even graduate from high school.

One of America's biggest problems is the large number of youngsters who never graduate from high school, or even attend many of the last few grades. A recent survey showed an average graduation rate of only 80 percent. That means about 775,000 children each year do not graduate, although some of those do get an equivalency degree later on. However, the graduation rate is only 68 percent for Blacks and 76 percent for Hispanics, while Whites and Asians have rates of 85 percent and 93 percent respectively. Because those are annual figures, the greater significance is that every ten years over seven million youngsters enter the adult population without a high school degree. This situation is one of the many creating unemployment and income inequality.

In total, America may have forty million people without a high school or an equivalency degree. Some of these are recent immigrants, but they are primarily the kids who grew up in toxic environments, where many are abused, are subject to unusual violence in the home or community, or are even homeless or in juvenile detention. Clearly, they received little or no benefit from their environment or the culture they were born into. If this is happening in one of the freest and most affluent societies in the world, it raises questions about just how good is a democracy. Or, it confirms that ours is truly a declining democracy.

If there is one single biggest cause of income inequality it is the fact that this 20 percent of our youth grow up with very little of the benefits they are due from a family and its community. Giving them welfare benefits now and throughout their lives may keep some from going hungry, but it is the dysfunctional culture and failed families that they are born into that create the problem—and no amount of money will ever fix that problem; it will just get worse as the numbers affected increase. That's what has been going on for the last fifty years. It is why the War on Poverty has failed, and it helps explain why income inequality has been steadily getting worse.

This sad situation is not caused by Big Oil, or the giant pharmaceutical companies, or even the crooks in government or the banks too big to fail. The despair of this growing group is the result of harmful ideas and attitudes introduced into our culture during the last sixty years by the opinion leaders of the country. The same plague has infected the mature democracies of Europe. Theodore Dalrymple is a noted physician who has treated the denizens of inner cities around the world and he has written on this modern curse. He is not as shocked by the poverty and ailments of his patients as he is by the absurd notions

in their minds that have filtered down from the intelligen-
tsias: that the poor are helpless victims, cursed by the powerful, and in need of constant assistance.[5]

Dalrymple explains in his book, *Life at the Bottom*, how
modern liberal ideologues have encouraged dependency
and rewarded bad behavior. Our culture now supports the
acceptability of helplessness, seeking victims who come
to believe that the government is both able and obliged to
cure their needs.

America's original culture called for the best in its
people. The fact that new political and cultural forces no
longer do that is a clear sign that our country's future is in
danger. A new concept of helplessness has been allowed
to shape our people's minds. The professional politicians
who run our nation have actually helped promote this new
cowardly way of thinking—they tell us we are "victims"
and promise to take care of everyone. In the recent debates
between the two Democrats, the main "issues" for Mr.
Sanders and Ms Clinton concerned which one would give
away the most goodies to the voters! Of course, they just
want to get enough votes to hold onto or improve their
cushy seats in Washington. But the result is that instead of
being uplifted, the people become discouraged, class divisions get larger, and inequality increases—the very things
that destroy a democracy.

Chapter 3

MEASURING PEOPLE - WHAT'S GOOD?

Think of this: If everyone in a community just took care of himself or herself and did little or no harm to others, what a fine place that would be to live! There would be little crime, empty jails, and small relief rolls. And imagine what it would be like if all members of a society avoided harming others, and also contributed in some meaningful way by means of their work and positive social behavior. That would be a utopia! But note that such a utopia would be one that was created by the people. A government can never create a utopia, only the people in a society can do that.

But leaders in government have a choice: They can either pursue policies that encourage the people to honor the civic virtues essential for a decent society or they can display gross dishonesty and avarice by their own behavior and encourage cheating and dependency in the public's behavior. Ours for the most part pursue the cheating and lying path. That is why America is in trouble! It's not the "people;" it's the people in government! That is why we must find ways to measure a person's capability better than we have in the past. We can't keep electing political hacks, with no management experience, and expect them to do anything good!

During this 2016 election campaigning, some candidates have boasted of his or her political "experience," and gullible voters have bought that claim. But, consider that point closely—do years spent in leadership roles give a candidate an advantage in dealing with future crises? Perhaps, but only if the person demonstrated real success during that period. Would you trust a coach who had thirty years of experience managing a baseball team but had a terrible win-loss record? Would a team even keep such a coach for more than a couple years? Certainly not! What if that coach promised to do this and that to make next year a winning year? Would you swallow that promise? Would you wonder why this and that hadn't been done somewhere in the last thirty years? How can an "experienced" leader promise reforms when she or he has been in power during the period that needs reforming? Obviously, by promising fixes, such a person is condemning her own record!

Assume further that the coach's actual record of "experience" includes a lot of obfuscation, deceit, gross payola, and cover-ups. Any rational measurement of a long-term sub-par *and* corrupt performance should conclude, "no more!" But, re-electing dishonest and faulty leaders has become a standard of today's partisan politics.

An ideal community is envisaged by the Golden Rule: "Do unto others as you would they do to you." But in America today, we are tearing down all reminders of historic guides to behavior; apparently some people are offended by the need to be nice!

There are no statistics I could find on this, but in America today there must still be a majority of people who live by our traditional ideas of responsibility and fair play as asked for in the Golden Rule and the Ten Commandments. That type of guidance to regulate man's behavior dates back almost four thousand years and has been used as a standard in most of the few free and successful nations in history. If America abandons such guides, what new standard is there to replace them? How can a people maintain their decency when a new governing elite supports the idea that morality is relative, moral behavior optional, and blurs its people's understanding as to what's right and what's wrong?

John Wooden, the "winningest coach" in history, who led the legendary UCLA basketball team in the 1970s, built his own life, and guided his players' conduct, with rules to live a "good life." Philosophers and some intellectuals and academics debate what "good" means, and confuse the dickens out of simple language, but Gooden, and his dad, made it look easy: the coach got his understanding of "good" and his strong moral base, as many do, from listening to his parent's advice. In his book, *The Essential Wooden*, he tells the reader that when he first went to school, his dad gave him a slip of paper, and said, Just follow these rules, Johnny, and you'll do all right. The slip contained just a few lines: "Never lie, never cheat, never steal." Then when he reached the ninth grade, his dad gave him another slip of paper with a little more advice: "Don't whine, don't complain, don't make excuses, and you'll be OK."[6] It's remarkable how a simple good person can say, concisely, what over educated great thinkers like Plato, Kant, and Rousseau couldn't manage in five hundred pages of confused musings!

Wooden, and his dad, didn't discover these "rules" of behavior, but they did find a way to apply them in a way that others would adopt. Such basic rules have been seen throughout history and in many cultures. We ignore them at our own risk. But most of our leaders in Washington break each rule every day! Who's worse: them, or us for electing them?

Coach Wooden brought his moral ideas to his coaching job. And he was clear about what values counted, identifying the fifteen personal traits that every person should develop. He listed those fifteen ethical precepts in "The Pyramid of Success." Making people strive to meet fifteen difficult personal goals may not sound popular, but by bringing his personal integrity and fine character to his job he provided useful guidance to all the kids in his care, and as a role model, earned the love and respect of his players. Most people recognize that your personal values affect your job performance. But, how often do our leaders in Washington try and excuse their personal corruption by saying it doesn't hurt their job performance? Too often, unfortunately; but maybe that's because they understand that lying and cheating IS actually their main job!

In Wooden's Pyramid, the two cornerstones are Industriousness and Enthusiasm. Completing the foundation of the pyramid are Friendship, Loyalty and Cooperation. On the sides are ten words, including Ambition, Honesty and Integrity, and at the top, Faith and Patience undergird the goal of Competitive Greatness. Wooden's objective was to direct his players into a "good" life based on those values that can empower all individuals. The pyramid, by its confirmation that a person can shape his own character, is a testament to the idea of free will, and the essential belief that with self control and persistence you can do a lot with however little your genes provided.

Most of the fifteen "good" behavior traits shown in the pyramid were taught by parents to their children in the past to help them become decent adults. But, with almost half of our nation's children now illegitimate, many with absent fathers, or a series of "stepfathers," such lessons are not taught to a growing portion of Americans. How can we expect another Great Generation when neither parents nor schools teach the basic requirements needed to live in a free society? Everyone thinks that ISIS and al Qaeda are the biggest threats to our future. But they should think again; our worst enemies are here at home.

Human nature, like most subjects in the soft-sciences, deals with living beings rather than inanimate objects. Because we are living beings with free will, our behavior is not subject to the same degree of certainty that physical scientists can ascribe to the movement of heavenly bodies. In spite of this unpredictable variability, there are some scholars who advance the idea that everything in life is pre-determined. They argue we are just naked apes and every-thing we ever do is predetermined by our genes and basic selfish animal natures. But Coach Wooden proved that with a little guidance and a lot of determination each of us can perfect both our skills and our character.

Thus, we know that a person's future is not predeter-mined but is subject to constant change. For that reason isn't it wise to recognize that people can change direction and do a better job of fulfilling their hopes and dreams? And doesn't that mean we should change our thinking about people and start thinking about how to bring out the best in them?

A willingness to deal with uncertainty is too often absent in the soft-sciences. For example, those who scream alarms about the imminent dangers of climate change or argue that it is settled science or "scientifically proven," will not admit to any uncertainty, even though everyone knows that weather forecasting, like economic forecasting is not even a true physical science. Chaos theory has shown that when there are a great number of variables and their accurate measurement is impossible, predictions cannot be accurate, but are simply suppositions.[7]

For our purposes, we must understand that human behavior is also a soft-science and subject, for the most part, to the vagaries of chaos theory! That is probably why there has been so little progress in measuring people. All we can say is that one's genes, one's environment, and one's own free will and tenacity, over time, will combine to shape an individual. Thus, the future of any child cannot be predicted at birth. Indeed, some studies show that even at twelve years of age a child's future success in life remains uncertain.

Although the existence of the bell-shaped curve is fraught with political freight, there is a measurable group of specific attributes in individuals based on their genes. If one did not inherit a high degree of eye-hand coordination, it will take an extraordinary amount of practice and training to get a job as a second baseman at Fenway Park! Practice will enhance skills, but there is a limit. As Michael Jordan demonstrated, hitting a 96 MPH fastball is beyond the wildest dreams of 99.999 percent of all human beings. But it does seem clear that, even for people with significant natural talent in a particular field, it will still require ten thousand hours of effective practice to become great. That is why such characteristics as persistence, emotional control, and patience are such an important part of each of us, and also explains why those critical qualities should be valued and measured just as much as a child's ability to add and subtract.

If we hope to understand and deal with income inequality in America we must understood more about what makes people different and how those differences might be measured. In *Wasted Genius*, an earlier book by this author, a formal method was outlined to measure a person's total competency. The idea grew out of the well known weakness of IQ and SAT test scores that simply reward abstract thinkers with good memories and a fair facility at arithmetic. But those mental gymnastics abilities represent only a couple of the dozens of important traits that make people competent adults who can function successfully in the modern world.

People born with the type of brain that gets good grades at school, and test well, are given every advantage, get into the top colleges, and snare the best jobs. Such preference for a limited competency is both unfair and also unwise, because many more competent individuals are not given equal opportunity. Talk about inequality! The failure to fully measure people results in gross inequality of opportunity for our youth.

Affirmative action plans have been used in recent years to provide a degree of equality for those people that have low school and test grades. The justification was that some minority students have been deprived of many cultural advantages and therefore score poorer than those with such advantages. That may be true, but the government should not pursue "preferential politics" that gives an advantage to favored groups. There can be no justice in such action—it creates an unfairness that affects people of all races and religions. Educators should have known better. After all, there are members of majority groups that also score low and deserve an equality of opportunity. That is why a form of affirmative action should be applied to everyone—not just a minority or racial group.

If educators love diversity so much they should welcome a class that is diversified and distinguished by having an over-all high level of positive character traits, not just test scores, but qualities such as imagination, persistence, drive, and self-reliance. And they should include B and C students who history has shown will be the creators of America's new businesses.

An undue emphasis on IQ and SAT scores may be helpful for those that pursue the hard sciences where such skills are all-important. An engineer must master many highly technical challenges to minimize the chance that his or her bridges and skyscrapers will fall down. But such technical virtuosity is less important for those pursuing the soft sciences. In those fields a host of other capabilities are all-important.

It is well known that most small businesses are created by average students who seem to possess many of the essential traits that are not measured by one's high school grades.[8] And, all the jobs in America come from those new enterprises that such "average" individuals create. The intellectually gifted, outside the hard-science arena, do not have any significant advantage unless they have a number of the other vital traits that make for success. That is why you occasionally read how an "A" student from Harvard has a lower level job than a "C" student from the community college. That is also why *every* child should be given an equal opportunity to succeed. Of all the virtues, we must emphasize fairness and justice to all, including people of all abilities.

In subsequent chapters we will examine the personal traits that add to a person's "total competency." For now, let's simply agree that each person is unique, not equal to anyone else, and can be measured as to his or her possibilities. Recent unfortunate cultural trends, led by a pervasive and destructive "political correctness," have precluded any attempt to apply a yardstick to individuals. In an effort to be non-judgmental, they proclaim that all people are equal, and some supposedly brilliant people even argue that we all deserve equal results. That, by the way, is a totally new concept—for two thousand years, many people have believed that Saint Peter, at the gates of heaven, holds his yardstick readily at hand to measure those who can come in and who cannot. We just should make sure that the measurement is of character and initiative, not test scores or ethnicity.

Chapter 4

MEASURING GOVERNMENTS - WHAT'S GOOD?

I f you want to help save America's democracy it is essential to start by thinking about what kind of country you want and what direction we should take to fix our stagnating economy and crippled government. While it is possible for philosophers and intellectuals to debate this question, most people would define a "good" government as one that provides several essential features for its people:

1) First comes security, the safety of the citizenry and their property. That is what allows an accumulation of infrastructure and personal wealth to continue for an extended time. (Most of the poverty in Africa (and some of our inner cities) is caused by the lack of order and safety for its people.)

2) Second comes the liberty and freedom of the people, the assurance that they can lead their lives as they choose, free from the tyranny of others or the government. (Most of the backwardness of totalitarian states comes from the lack of personal freedom and motivation.)

3) Third comes freedom of thought and speech—the right for people to believe and say what they choose, free from oppression or sanction. New ideas and innovation depend on open communication. (The lack of innovation in Communist Russia and most of the Middle East was caused by the censorship of new ideas.)

4) Fourth comes the opportunity for self-fulfillment that comes from an empowering culture that encourages the initiative of its people to pursue their goals. Governments must reward good behavior and be tough on bad behavior. (Most populist democracies and socialist nations provide so many benefits to the needy that their working population become overly taxed, overly regulated, and discouraged.)

5) Fifth, comes an open and free economy that allows everyone an equal opportunity of achieving self-sufficiency, with a level playing field for all. (There are very few places in the world that allow free and fair opportunity to all their people.)

6) Sixth, comes the support of institutions that provide the protection of a fair legal and judicial system, and an easily entered but well regulated financial system that protects private property, upholds business contracts, and provides adequate banking services. (In much of the world people have no access to deeds for their property and no ability to sell or borrow on their assets.)

These six attributes of a good government provide for the freedom, safety, and maximum opportunity for its people. They are what Professor Dershowitz has called "negative rights." They prevent any outside forces from acting in a negative, or harmful way to limit the activity of individuals. They are enshrined in the Bill of Rights attached to the American Constitution. They are an integral part of a free enterprise economy which requires certain institutional supports that help people do business in a safe and efficient manner. But, none of them are "positive rights" which grant each citizen a plethora of tangible gifts from the government. There was never any attempt to guarantee positive rights to our people. There is no free lunch. Isn't safety, liberty, and opportunity enough?

It is known that for liberty to exist, people must take responsibility for themselves; they must endeavor to be self-sufficient and independent, for as soon as they accept assistance, they lose their independence. The price you must pay for freedom is to take care of yourself and your family. Once you take aid, the government will restrict how you spend it. (No soda pop, no cigarettes) Once you take medical services, they will limit your usage. (They can pull the plug!) Once you take disability insurance you can't work or play (Do you like faking it that much?) Once you take housing, they will tell you where to live. (Do you really like Section 8 condos?)

Found politicians grist for his humor-Grouch Marx

In order for a nation's people to resist the temptation of accepting alms they need a culture that encourages self-sufficiency, honesty, and at least a little grit. But the problem is: how do you separate the truly needy and deserving from the undeserving? One way would be to apply sound management principles: close the hundreds of existing aid programs, and design one well controlled agency to manage the job. It can be done, and must be done, because with over a third of our population receiving some form of assistance we have gone too far!

That brings us to a seventh element in "good government," and it is sort of a positive right—the provision of some assistance to those victims of natural disasters and personal misfortune. It represents an exception to the rule that only negative rights should be granted to citizens. Indeed, some historians have tied the success of Western civilization to its unique provision of aid to help the victims of disasters and thereby strengthen and support individuals where most needed. There is truly a need for a safety-net, in spite of the prices one pays when accepting aid. But that assistance should be parceled out carefully and not so liberally as to seduce more and more people into dependency. There has to be a place for tough love in the granting of assistance lest the ranks of disabled and unemployed become a majority! There also needs to be justice—to ensure that aid only goes to the most deserving.

It is self evident that democracies will be in danger once their financially assisted rolls approach 50 percent of their people. Nations with such a large proportion of dependents are often called "populist democracies," and that's another way of saying that they are past their peak, and on the decline. It's just simple arithmetic, albeit in fractions and percentages: Less than half a country's population cannot long support themselves as well as all the other half. But when half have decided it's better to just take aid rather than earn it, a corner has been turned. As Margaret Thatcher told us, "Socialism is great till you run out of other people's money!" As a side note here, there is considerable evidence that

America may have reached that point. We are giving aid even to non-citizens—illegal aliens who have broken our laws! The question is: how do we go back? How do we escape the usual fate of a populist democracy?

Number five above deserves special attention because one of our biggest failings is in the requirement that there be a fair and level playing field for all people. In business organizations it is an accepted rule that if an employee is to be held responsible for something, that person has to be given a reasonable chance to achieve success, and more specifically, that person must be given the authority needed to accomplish the tasks assigned.

★ ★ ★ ★ ★ ★ ★ ★ ★

"Politics is the art of looking for trouble, finding it everywhere, diagnosing it incorrectly, and applying the wrong remedies."

---Groucho Marx

★ ★ ★ ★ ★ ★ ★ ★ ★

Since it is assumed that all people in a democracy will do their best to care for themselves and their families it is the height of cruelty and folly to set up roadblocks for some, and an open road to riches for others. That is plain unfair; maybe it's just a "tilt" in pinball, but it's a catastrophic failing in governing a free nation. A government that plays favorites, granting benefits to some and not others, is doomed sooner or later to be ruined by these injustices. Isn't such an unjust government the same as a father who favors one child over another?

A good government, like a parent, has to promote and support a culture that values fair play, honesty, and keeping promises. Otherwise it is merely operating as an emperor in disguise. And czars, sultans, and emperors never led the type of successful free nation that America symbolizes. In other words, governing officials can't expect to cheat, lie, steal, and play favorites if they expect the best from their people. A nation's leaders must lead by example—by being honest and maintaining a level playing field where everyone has the same opportunities. John Adams stated this principle at the very beginning of our nation, in 1798, speaking to the officers of a Massachusetts militia:

> "We have no government armed with the
> power capable of contending with human pas-
> sions, unbridled by morality and true reli-
> gion. Our constitution is made only for a
> moral and religious people. It is wholly inad-
> equate to the government of any other."
> John Adams, to the officers of the First Brigade,
> Third Division, Massachusetts
> Militia, October 11, 1798.

There you have it—our government is not suited to govern the existing changed population! America started with, and was primarily built by reasonable and honorable people and its culture supported such values for a long-time. This was generally true up until about World War II, when the Greatest Generation went willingly off to war to defend the liberty of others. But since then, doesn't it seem that our leaders have set an example of corruption, outright lying, handing out special favors, confusing the issues with political spin, creating loopholes for a select few, and using regulatory power to abuse those not in favor?

In governance, the people chosen to lead are supposed to be better than most, more experienced, more trustworthy, smarter, and more honorable. The great leaders of the past led by example, inspiring their public to a loftier level of conduct. Today's leaders for the most part do the opposite, demonstrating by their own actions, that lying and cheating is not only acceptable, but what everyone does. Isn't it fair to say that most of the people you know are more trustworthy and honest than the people in Washington that are entrusted to run the country? Isn't it true that character counts? When voting, shouldn't we measure the candidates and look for a high level of personal integrity as well as managerial competence?

The ever-increasing corruption in American government is creeping up on us and threatening to end our long and unparalleled success story. In fact, the recent conduct of our executive, judicial, and congressional branches of government have worked against each of the six things a good government should provide that we listed at the beginning of this chapter. Instead they have set up road-blocks for some, and made loopholes for others. They have fiddled with bank mortgages and the money supply, bringing on the disastrous melt-down of 2008, they opened the floodgates of "benefits," with no controls and no concern over justice or costs, so that our nation's finances are close to bankruptcy. What is supposed to function as a "safety-net" has become a way of life, an offering to be scammed by some, a positive right for others to escape responsibility.

Is it possible that our elected leaders actually seek to make everyone dependent on the government? To lead us into dependency? That way America would have to be run *by* the elite and *for* the elite. If so, Huxley's vision of a drugged electorate is already here.

It might be instructive to remember that the president is head of the *executive* department, and holds a *management* position. The president's job description calls for the efficient management and supervision of all the federal agencies that spend trillion dollar budgets and employ a couple million workers. The president is not the pastor in chief, or a social worker, or a psychiatrist, or a social coordinator. The job calls for someone both experienced and capable in management skills.

In order to oversee this huge bureaucracy the president must appoint experienced administrators to every top executive post, not the political hacks that we usually see heading the cabinet posts. In short, if the chief executive would just concentrate on managing the government bureaucracy and set aside the ideological battles, America would be better off, and might even be great again!

Our task is not to assign blame to either the people who vote or the people who get elected. The objective must be to fix what is wrong, and neither political party seems to have any interest in that solution! Every two years, the candidates in the political debates argue forever about how they plan to tweak this law or that law to cure our problems! But we all know that the past fifty years of tweaks have not helped, and, in fact have probably done more harm than good. Poverty has remained the same and income inequality has gotten worse.

The Washington establishment is firmly in place, resistant to change, and leading us down the path to destruction. The only change we ever see is the need to spend more money. Most newcomers to Washington are quickly controlled by the establishment in place. It will take a proven administrator, with no obligation to special interests, and with the strength and determination to knock some heads, if we are to restore America's exceptional virtue and strength.

PART II
WHAT IS SO SPECIAL ABOUT HUMAN BEINGS?

Chapter 5

WHAT MAKES US UNIQUE
THE BACKGROUND OF MODERN MAN

The story of equality and inequality starts way back with the origin of the first modern humans who suddenly appeared in South Africa and were marked by an unusually large brain, upright stature, a prominent forehead, and a height very close to ours. Those distinctive features gave them a huge competitive advantage in survival over all other creatures. If we examine the varying paths those first people followed, we can gain a better understanding of today's people, as well as how and why we are so unique and different from each other.

It was only about seventy thousand years ago that these modern humans started their migration out of Africa and spread across most of the world's lands. They were unique beings in the world, possessing anatomical features that provided them with speech, and an ability to fashion sophisticated tools, art, and eventually, as their numbers grew, large organized societies. They first arrived in Europe about thirty-five thousand years ago, and reached northern Asia, the Pacific islands, and the Americas about twenty to thirty thousand years ago.

"If I have seen further, it is by standing

On the shoulders of giants."

Isaac Newton, 1676

Modern science tells us that these people, newly arrived on the scene, were fully developed along the lines of modern man when they left Africa, possessing roughly the same speaking ability and thinking processes that we do today! The migrations and identity of these people has been fairly well mapped by the use of DNA and carbon testing of fossil remains. It was their unique anatomy and the power of speech that helped them start the social and technical advances that have led to the modern world.

Colin Renfrew suggests that all these people possessed the innate genetic and physical capacity to conceive of and make useful shelters and tools but that the extra ingredient propelling their advance was that they learned how to accumulate and transmit such know-how. The power of speech and later the use of writing allowed individuals to train each new generation. Acquired knowledge cannot be passed on genetically, in the DNA of the parents to that of the children, and that is why all animals, and some human groups, have never advanced from their earliest levels. But modern humans were able to pass on learned skills orally, at first, and later, most people developed written records.

In that way all prior skills could be learned by each new generation, allowing them to discover new truths by building on previous discoveries. This process was recognized as the key element in human progress by those people who launched Western Europe into the Industrial Revolution. Leading pioneers in science often attributed their success to the discoveries of prior scientists. One of the first to do so was Bernard of Chartres in the twelfth century, which is an indication of the early scientific progress in Europe. But its most familiar roots in English appeared in a 1676 letter of Isaac Newton. It is that written record of past discoveries that allows today's high school science student to acquire, in just four years, the accumulated discoveries of the last four thousand years!

However, the extraordinary accomplishments that created human progress could occur only in societies where there were schools and universities, the safety to study, students motivated to learn, and teachers free to teach.

Those requirements have been absent in many nations since time began, and are currently absent even in many areas of America. Where those cultural boosts are absent you should expect very poor success rates, whether it is in sub-Saharan Africa or America's rural and urban ghettos.

During mankind's slow and gradual gathering of knowledge, the gifted individuals that pioneered each new discovery, as well as all those who employed the new technologies, were probably among the more successful citizens and thus were more successful at surviving and passing on their genes. It is believed by many that the human race gained cognitive capabilities, not so much from evolutionary mutations, as from the relatively high fertility of successful people—being successful, they probably reared more children to adulthood than the less successful.

It is significant that for the last few thousand years, survival of the fittest has not been about surviving an adverse mother nature, but about favoring the reproduction of those people most adept at dealing with evolving social systems. This process had little to do with Darwinian evolution, which has been minimal in the last ten thousand years, but everything to do with some people raising more offspring than others. This genetic improvement would have had a cumulative effect in advancing societies where the increasingly competitive challenges would have created an ever-escalating selection process. In those places, the populations gained competencies not needed or valued in stagnant communities that had little writing or organizing activity.

The advance from hunter-gatherers to pastoral and agricultural ages marked the beginnings of recorded history and led to the earliest civilizations we see in ancient China and the Middle East. The societies that developed agricultural practices benefitted in two ways: They had a more plentiful food supply that accommodated rapid population growth and the developing need for storage and inventories of grain led to the use of symbols to keep track of supplies.

In the Middle East, the Sumerians and Assyrians over three thousand years ago made the initial use of cuneiform symbols, which were also developed in a few other locales around the world. The modern alphabet came later from the Phoenicians and Greeks almost three thousand years ago. Renfrew refers to this development of writing as the culmination of the symbolic advances when early man made giant steps forward. However, many societies never went beyond the most basic forms of writing and a few isolated societies never even got to the most primitive forms of writing. Is it really convincing to say that the culture of a society that never developed any form of writing is the equal of one that did?

A further advance in human cognition was seen in regions where the people went beyond the symbolic phase of writing to a theoretic stage which enabled individuals to solve theoretic questions about such phenomena as the movement of solid objects, the logic of geometry, and how magnetism and electricity operate.[9] Such advances of the theoretic stage relied on a significant refinement of written records and are seen only in those parts of the world where writing and schooling had advanced to a high level.

These varying developments as modern man moved throughout the world explain much of the different trajectories of human development. As Renfrew observes, "There was no one generalized story of human progress, no uniform pattern of development."[10] The unknown is why, if they were all of equal cognitive potential, did some people never develop any use of writing? And why did so many, even with writing skills, never develop mechanical and technological skills?

Professor Renfrew asserts that all these modern humans who dispersed out of Africa over fifty thousand years ago were very closely related, and still are, because only superficial differences in appearance have evolved since that time. "A child born today...would be very little different in its DNA—that is in the genotype—and hence in innate capacities from one born fifty thousand years ago."[11] Renfrew goes on to write that all the varied changes in prosperity, behavior, customs, and learning "cannot be explained by any inherent or emerging genetic changes...

Modern molecular genetics suggests that, apart from the normal distribution range present in all populations in matters such as IQ, all humans are equal."[12]

Now this is a wonderful statement and suggests the equality of all races and ethnic groups. However, how can we agree with the professor on the equality of competency when we know that people are different, some are better than others in all sorts of ways, and others are less competent than others in many ways?

Renfrew's phrase must be examined more closely for what it doesn't say. It states only that there is very little difference between human beings and that we all have roughly comparable cognitive potential. Now if you take two similar automobiles, with the same horsepower motor and similar wheel bearings and weight, they may be thought of as having roughly the same potential. But if one has better fuel, more thorough oiling and greasing, perhaps an afterburner, or goosed up torque, it may be the superior car. And if its driver is more daring, more skilled, and experienced, it will probably win the race.

Thus having very similar DNA does not make people equal. And having anatomically similar brains does not make people equal in abilities. This should be obvious because we all may have similar brain structures, but I know that there are those who are more competent than me. If their brain is built the same as mine, what makes them smarter?

Let's also question the "normal distribution range" he refers to which is a more politically correct way of referring to the bell curve. From statistics we know that within any group, individuals can be ranked along a bell curve from left to right, as worse or better at whatever function is being measured. If it's height, the people of average height will be clustered in the middle, and the shorter or taller ones will appear in declining numbers, at each side. Now, if all bell curves, for all categories measured, were of the same shape, it would be easy to compare groups. But there is no "normal" distribution or bell curve. The bells vary in height, slope, and width. The point is that although all people may have a similar brain structure, results can vary greatly in actual practice. Theory depends on averages, but reality relies on the actual distribution. If one group is not a purely average selection, it can be better or worse than another group in many ways.

If you took at a random group of men from Kenya and matched them in a marathon with a similar random group taken from Newton, Massachusetts, which group would win? Most people would go with the Kenyans because in that skill one group probably is superior to the other. If such differences in long-distance running abilities are so clear, why don't we accept the fact that there are many other differences too?

A further gap in Professor Renfrew's assertion is the qualification that we are "of roughly the same cognitive potential." Now you can take two individuals with roughly the same cognitive potential and immerse them in advanced mathematical studies until they are twenty years old and when tested in trigonometry and calculus one will probably do much better than the other. Small differences in mental processing power impact people assaulting the barriers of higher math just as different types of cognitive talent influence who succeeds at astro-physics and who is totally befuddled!

Most of my college classmates were of roughly equal mental ability, with similar SAT scores and similar IQ scores, but only a handful, perhaps less than 5 percent, could fathom higher mathematics and physics. Our DNA may have been similar, but somewhere, something unmeasured in the way their minds worked, gave them special skills the rest of us most clearly lacked.

Renfrew wrote some years ago, and as proof that there is no such thing as "settled science," recent genomic discoveries have shed new light on this subject. The new findings have shown that we are not all as similar as previously believed. We have until now assumed that the human genome, or "book of life," is largely the same for everyone.

But it turns out that on our individual DNA strands, entire sentences or even whole pages are repeated a different number of times for each person. Instead of humanity being almost identical, as previously believed, there are very large biological differences between each of us. This provides an entirely new insight into why we vary so much not only in personality traits and abilities, but in our tendency to specific diseases.

The bottom line is that once mankind advanced sufficiently in skills to overcome nature, environmental conditions became less important in selecting what types of people would succeed. With the advent of writing and large communities, a population had to develop new abilities for working effectively in large groups and applying the latest ideas in organization and governance. The hunter-gatherers were gradually replaced by the "organization man" and a new set of valuable traits were called forth. Civilization then advanced rapidly as those most adept at working in large educated societies passed on their genes to succeeding generations. Evolution caused few changes in humans but the genetic transmission of certain superior attributes were inevitable due to differing fertility rates. That selection process at work not only increased the inequality of mankind but created wide differences in the capabilities of those living in different societies.

Chapter 6

THE TWENTY-FIVE YEAR FACTOR; APPRENTICES AND ACHIEVING ADULTHOOD

One of the most unique things about humans is that it requires twenty-five years for their brains to fully form. The pre-frontal cortex, the part of the brain that helps you control impulsive behavior and to think logically, remains a work in progress for that long. Insurance companies and rental car operators are very aware of this delayed maturity and that is why their rates are higher for everyone twenty-five or younger. It's all because of our biology; just the way we are made; your pre-frontal cortex does not become fully developed until you're twenty-five. That's why the army always drafted eighteen year olds, who mistakenly tended to believe that war would be exciting!

Dan Coyle has written extensively on just why we develop so slowly and why training and intense participation is required to fully develop one's potentials. He describes the vital role of myelin, a gray sheath that forms around the body's neurons and enhances the transmission of the signals that govern most of our thinking and actions.[13] It represents part of the reason humans are so superior to all other living forms. We are born with limited skills, but our bodies gradually develop extraordinary amounts of competencies as called for as we learn to cope with the world around us. The development of thick layers of myelin is generated by the efforts made to adapt to that environment. The more you use all those neurons, the better the myelin becomes.

In children, myelin arrives in a series of waves, the volume based on one's genes and the amount of activity expended. A rapid accumulation persists into young adulthood and then slows down. During one's teens and early twenties, the brain is extraordinarily receptive to learning new skills, but the amount of gain is in proportion to the application applied to such learning. Children that are allowed to waste this precious period in idle pursuits will develop their capabilities less than those who engage actively in the world around them. Adults retain the ability to add myelin throughout their life, but it accumulates much slower. If you have tried to learn a language, scientific studies, mathematics, or a musical instrument late in life you will realize how hard it has become to master any new subject. That is why it is such a terrible waste of a young life for parents to let their kids wallow in idleness or careless diversions. That is just one more example of how kind intentions can create cruel results.

The delay in becoming fully rational is actually a blessing in disguise. We cannot within minutes of our birth leap to our feet and flee predators the way a gazelle can. But, our slow start does gradually ignite, and then off we go, to limits unknown to all other living creatures. Our brains are not pre-programmed, but are open and adaptable to whatever circumstances they encounter. They learn from experience, develop the ability to plan ahead, and change course, imagine abstractions and possibilities, and work strategically in creative ways.

But, twenty-five years! That's a third of one's life expectancy. It would have been over half the life expectancy of most humans until very recently. That long maturing process shows why family and culture are so significant in shaping each new generation. It is the family and community environment that you are exposed to during that long period that shapes who you become. And no wonder we end up very unequal, because humans around the country, and world, are exposed to every conceivable type of culture and family environment as they mature. It is inconceivable to believe that these very different cultures create adults with the same competency.

Because teenagers do not have the mature judgment that adults do is no reason to overprotect them. The ferment of hormones, the growing endocrine system, and a developing brain structure are what make them extremely receptive to life experiences. There will never be a period when they can gain so much ability. Although they may lack judgment and emotional control, this is nevertheless the time when they most need to be given the chance to assume responsibility, apply their best efforts and skills to tasks, and provide their brains with the challenges that, by adding layers and layers of myelin, will create the maximum growth in their competencies.

It is also a mistake to underestimate their ability just because they are not fully developed. Alexander the Great was about twelve when he tamed the wild stallion Bucephalus, and showing the same determination, ten years later, he rode the beast, leading his cavalry, and conquered most of the known world! And, nothing's changed—today we have dot-com billionaires less than twenty-five years old that are building empires in the Cloud. The twenty-five year rule doesn't mean kids are incompetent until then. It means that they benefit greatly and rapidly until that time.

It is unfortunate that today's parenting objectives are to prevent disappointments and reward children with a trophy regardless of actual accomplishment. Such parental zeal does more harm than good by denying the child real-world experiences, a chance to deal with disappointments, and savor truly earned successes. By creating sheltered, managed, and artificial environments parents prevent children from gaining the personal growth and maturity that they will need as adults. Instead of encouraging children to "grow up," parents hold them back. In fact, parents may keep their children from ever becoming adults at all! That is why there are so many books about "adult children" and "deferred adolescence!" By sheltering them from work experience, parents are imposing limits on the amount of growth that would otherwise be possible.[14]

Frank Furedi, professor of sociology at the University of Kent, says we have infantilized young people by sheltering them from responsibility and work. He calls it a cultural shift that allows adolescence to extend into a person's twenties and results in a passive dependence and immaturity rather than a seasoned adult. Social workers point to the diminished sense of personal responsibility that they see that results from this cultural change—we are hurting our children by letting them delay entry into the adult world.

During the eighteenth and nineteenth century, when America and Western European nations were forging ahead with the Industrial Revolution, much of the labor, and many of the innovations came from the hands and minds of apprentices and former apprentices. It was expected in the culture of that time that young boys, once they reached twelve to fourteen years of age, would be apprenticed out to a business or tradesman for seven or more years to earn their keep and learn a trade. That would usually mean leaving the family home and working long hours for a master, who wielded iron discipline and demanded respectful behavior.

The surprising thing about those apprentices is that many went on to become very significant in science, industry, and engineering. Samuel Smiles's book, *Lives of the Engineers*, tells the story of many boys who came from humble beginnings and, as a direct result of their childhood work and self-schooling, became famous engineers, chemists, and machinists who led most of the advances that built the Industrial Revolution. These were some of the key people of the Industrial Revolution in England and Scotland. America's own famed Benjamin Franklin spent years assigned to a print shop starting at the age of fourteen. After Thomas Edison was thrown out of school, he worked as a teletype operator as a teenager, and developed his remarkable aptitude for the newly emerging teletype technologies. Andrew Carnegie began his storied career as a teenager sweeping floors in a factory in Pittsburgh.

Apprentices received little schooling. Their education was to learn a trade and it was accomplished by performing the trade, starting at the lowest level and advancing as they developed skills. They filled a productive role, producing goods and services, at a very low cost and obtained an education from their work experience and by self-study. Compare that to today where a child is pampered, driven to pre-arranged sports, music, and dance events, and bought special clothing and gear for each such non-productive activity.

After all that coddling, America's upper and middle economic groups pay for many years of schooling, either through taxes or tuition payments, and over half of those children "study" such relatively useless subjects as anthropology, women's history, the environment, movies, and social psychology—then, after having wasted their most impor-

Left home for apprenticeship at fourteen years of age-Benjamin Franklin

tant formative years, they seem surprised that they can't get a decent job!

Meanwhile, the government has loaned them more than a trillion dollars in student loans to go to college. The majority never graduate. And they riot because they don't want to repay the loans, or they feel offended by what a fellow student or faculty member said, or because they object to some aspect of the school's educational and social stance. They have in effect been taught to fight over trivialities instead of learning something of value. Policy makers should think twice before financing eighteen year-olds in college to study some of the soft-sciences. They are merely encouraging deferred adolescence on a grand scale—harming our children in the process-and borrowing the money from China to do so!

Because America has become divided into a couple totally different cultures, the coddling applies to and harms only the more affluent. The less affluent are not harmed by such coddling, but get harmed even more from the poverty of their households and the truly helpless attitudes of many at the bottom. Many of these seriously neglected youth never even get the chance to contemplate college or moving up in the world they were born into. The promise of equal opportunity for all, that democracies are supposed to provide, has been denied for many by the policies pursued in Washington.

This chaotic situation does represent a sea change in culture, and to the extent that some children are short-changed, inequality grows. It should be obvious to all that kids are damaged from postponing the need to grow up or by being born illegitimate into single parent homes. Many are denied the challenging yet productive experience of entering the adult world of responsible self-reliant citizens; and, it is a certainty that both the kids and the nation suffer from this waste of all that young potential. An experienced manager, freed of all the ideological argumentation, and liberated from the nonsense promoted by teachers' unions and the education experts in the Department of Education, could reverse these unfortunate cultural shifts. For starters, a good manager would abolish the Department of Education and common core curricula, and incentivize the states to find better ways of teaching by matching financial aid to the participation rate of their youth. Barring such an effort, America's children will continue to receive less of what they need to strengthen themselves and the country.

Chapter 7

HOW CULTURE SHAPES INDIVIDUALS

The first thing to understand about *cultures* is that they don't just emerge suddenly out of thin air—they are formed by generations of people over hundreds, sometimes thousands of years, and can be modified by each new generation. Therefore, when someone says that culture shapes people, they really are saying that the prior generations that created the existing culture are the actual people shaping the generations that followed. Everything comes from human action![15]

The term "culture" refers to the traditions, customs, technologies, and organizational elements of a society. A culture goes beyond the mere mechanics of a society to influence the attitudes and beliefs of the people. Different cultures have been created by the various groups of people all around the world as they transitioned from hunter gatherers, to agricultural groups, and finally into today's more cosmopolitan and urban dwellers. Because cultures around the world have taken many different paths, the resulting cultures have achieved very different results.

This variation of cultures exists because different people in different locations created different forms of culture. Furthermore, some people have been more adept at adapting their cultures to changing circumstances; while in other places, cultures, whether good or bad, have remained relatively unchanged. But the bottom line is that cultures differ and some function for their people better than others.

Thus, a culture is not some mysterious force, some factor forced on humanity; it is simply a creation of the people in a given region who instituted the basic beliefs and attitudes of the culture and occasionally made adjustments to suit changing needs. And, some people did a better job of it than others. For example, the Islamic culture, dominated by a theocracy that resisted all attempts at reform, and denied many of the human rights that have been honored in Western nations, has held back its people for almost a thousand years.

The cultural failings under Islamic rule illustrate that, while it is a mistake to radically alter a successful culture, it can be equally disastrous to halt all change in a backward culture. It is this undeniable fact that cultures are man-made that leads Colin Renfrew to criticize Richard Dawkins's odd theory about "memes," a term that Dawkins coined as a substitute for cultural norms. The two men are in agreement that whether you call them memes or cultural norms, they played a major role in advancing or retarding mankind's progress. But their difference lies in the fact that Dawkins equates memes with biology and genetics. Thus, Dawkins refers to "cultural evolution" as a force comparable to genetic and evolutionary forces. Renfrew describes Dawkins's theory as simplistic and points out that it distorts the nature of culture, making it a force by itself, similar to biological evolution, which would falsely place it outside the control of humans.

Renfrew's objection is correct—genetic changes are based on natural selection of the fittest and reproductive/fertility success. It is not wholly under the control of the people involved. But culture is formed by humans and reflects the nature and belief systems of a population. It is developed and maintained by the conscious and considered action of individuals. A culture can be dramatically altered by deliberate human action.

Thus, evolution and genetic changes are a biological mechanism, while culture is man-made. By labeling culture as memes subject to evolution, Dawkins confuses this important distinction. He relies on the tortured concept that when cultural elements are copied and carried on by generations of humans, it proves that they exist for their own sake, and if those cultural elements can induce people to honor them, and pass them on to their children, they have succeeded in replicating themselves!

Only an intellectual could twist reality this way. It is like the way Lysenko argued that acquired habits could be passed on in the genes to one's children! If cultural norms continue over generations it is not because they have a life of their own and have reproduced themselves—it is simply because the people that live by them haven't yet modified them!

This fact that cultures are formed, by a society of people over hundreds of years, illustrates the need to know something about your history. It seems that many people today think that our American culture is just something that happened, that they were born into, and is owed no special respect or honor. They make two mistakes as a result of such ignorance: First, they fail to grasp that what was built by their predecessors, and bequeathed to us, is arguably the most successful, free, and prosperous culture in history, and therefore something to be protected and honored. Second, if they see what appears to them to be defects, they will willy-nilly pursue changes that might make things better, but in fact may do harm because they do not take into consideration the social and economic forces that have shaped the world we live in. Because American culture has worked better than any other in history, it is wise to think twice about changing it!

Sociologists have found that a nation's culture is an important part of its capital. Just as its people provide a nation's most valuable resource, their culture shapes and empowers each new generation of those people for better or worse. America's four hundred year-long meteoric success indicates that both its people and their culture were among the world's best. Those who built America to its current supremacy created a vital foundation, a strong cohesive culture, schools, churches, roads and factories, safe communities, and most importantly, a positive self-reliant attitude in its citizens. Failure to maintain that cultural foundation will lead to a declining society just as surely as will a neglected transport and industrial infrastructure. [16]

It is a common fault among great scholars and writers to downplay the role of human action in shaping our history. Even Adam Smith, who summarized how and why free enterprise works so well in some societies, suggested that there was "an invisible hand" that made capitalism function. Of course capitalism works only because the hands and minds of its multitude of participants make it work. If there is a "hand" involved, it is the many calloused hands of the workers that toil to produce the food and goods being bought and sold!

Suffice it to say that when it comes to cultures, some are good and some are bad. If you ever discuss "multiculturalism," remember that, as a compassionate human, you should respect all people but not necessarily their culture, for there are a number of awful cultures that condone shameful practices![17] For example, Muslim disregard for women's rights has been on full display in Europe lately where gangs of young Islamic men, recently arrived as refugees, have had the audacity to attack and molest women right on the streets of Europe's cities. Such unbelievable behavior raises serious doubts about whether such people could ever assimilate into Western democracies. And it underscores a growing belief that democracy and theocracy are so incompatible that they cannot co-exist within one nation.

The distinction between genes and culture is important because it explains that although Muslims and Christians may have possessed similar genes fifteen hundred years ago, their subsequent lives and prosperity have been primarily influenced by having constructed very different belief systems and very different governmental and religious institutions. The cultural developments forged within European societies during the last one thousand years obviously "worked" much more effectively than those of the Middle East. The people in the Middle East may once have had similar DNA to Europeans, but their culture and religion became vastly different, and therein lies the relative success stories of the two regions.

On this subject, consider the Protestant Reformation. In 1506AD, a lowly priest in medieval Germany, Martin Luther, declared his objections to the dominant Catholic Church's practices. He did so quite dramatically, nailing a list of ninety-five complaints about the church's conduct and teachings on the door of the All Saints' Church in Wittenberg, Germany. He endorsed a growing sentiment among the people of Western Europe that God and the Christian faith were available to every believer, without the intercession of priests, and that the entire culture of Catholicism had grown corrupt and had to be reformed.

Luther's posting caused a remarkable cultural revolution, and it led directly to the scientific vigor of the new Protestant denominations and spearheaded spectacular secular progress throughout Northern Europe. This huge shift in the way people thought and acted had nothing to do with evolution or genetic change. It was brought about by the action of a concerned human being, exercising his free will and determination to free his culture from a corrupt and restrictive straitjacket and move into an open and inquisitive way of life.

After Luther's remarkable impact on the cultures of northern Europe, the remaining Catholic countries of southern Europe were soon left behind in the race to the

Industrial Revolution. Here was a cataclysmic cultural impact, and it was clearly created by individual human action. It was unlike evolutionary or biological change which works slowly, in the background. And, by the way, the Islamic nations never benefitted from such a dynamic change to their culture because the Muslim clerics, who held dictatorial power, have always stifled the few individuals who sought reform. The culture of Islam creates a belief of helplessness among its people—they are taught that the clerics and Allah, their God, have total power over their lives. There is no provision for heroic individuals to act as they see best for they must obey the religion's rules. The literal meaning of "a Muslim," is "one who submits."

The fact that most Americans instinctively resist submission to any centralized authority dates back to the ancient Greeks. Homer's great epics about the ancient Greek people passed on a blessing to the West that empowered people to act heroically and not live passively. This tradition raises a question for today, in 2016: America has gradually become more and more stained by way too much income inequality, corruption at the very top, and a spiraling debt that threatens to bankrupt our states and the national government. Are the people of this great land going to submit to the power of the new elites that steal our liberty, our wealth, and our honor? Are we becoming like the Muslims, content to submit and accept whatever the leaders force on us?

In the past, America was built on the Judeo-Greek-Christian foundation of respect for the individual, his or her liberty, and his or her property. Our own revolution was sparked when King George merely imposed a few relatively small tariffs and restrictions on our shipping. Those rebels didn't know the meaning of "submit." Think how they would react today to all the executive orders flowing from the White House or the commands of government agencies enforcing millions of rules and regulations!

America's founders had to have been some of the most independent people in history! Very few of the rest of the world's people ever showed such spirit—because their culture and religion held them back. The Eastern philosophies and religions, such as Confucianism, Buddhism, and Hinduism, had a common denominator in their teaching-to live orderly lives, to not rock the boat, and to look for inner peace and contentment. There are very few rebels living in those cultures. Indeed, the way to improve your lot under the Hindu faith is to be quiet and hope to earn a better life in the afterlife! So you don't come back as a snake!

How many Westerners would fall for that line? What would Sam Adams, John Wayne, Martin Luther, Ulysses, or Rosa Parks do if asked to keep quiet and accept their lot in life? Where would Western civilization be if its people and culture had just meekly accepted their lot in life? But they didn't do that. Instead they shaped and manipulated their culture so that it helped them move forward instead of holding them back. But that's the past. Our enabling culture was shaped and developed in that creative fashion up to recent times; but today, American culture is under attack.

Our president travels the world and apologizes for America! Candidates for national office want to turn us into a socialist state with free everything for everybody. Our political and academic elites have imposed a new mind-numbing political correctness that outlaws the discussion of anything they don't like. There are attorney generals in some states that are seeking to prosecute individuals who deny some of the claimed elements of Global Warming. Our kids are being taught a new cultural norm that embraces a hedonistic moral relativism, an approval of all cultures whether admirable or horrific, and an unthinking toleration for everything that is destroying all standards of behavior and responsibility. It actually may be that we will wish Dawkins was right and that our culture was imprinted like a genetic stamp on America. But, that is not the case; there are people at work seeking to totally transform America, and we better keep them away from the reins of power.

Chapter 8

THE NATURE NURTURE DEBATE

There should be little debate or controversy here. The simple truth is that people are born with their parents' genetics, and they are raised in the culture that their parents and communities provide. The "experts" have wasted a lot of their readers' time by writing books that argue whether nature or nurture is the major determinant in our lives. The simple fact is that each child is "stuck" with whatever genes he or she inherited, but that individual will be shaped either favorably or unfavorably by the nurturing received. The only thing under parental control, aside from mate selection, is the nurturing and environment they provide to guide their children into adulthood. Unfortunately it is in the provision of an empowering and nurturing environment to American youth where we see an ever expanding failure.

It is a mistake to think of a culture or the environment as a single force because they have many parts, and some parts are more under our control than others. A person may not be able to establish a perfect world for their children to grow up in, but they can do quite a bit: the family structure, the choice of schools, the neighborhood, the availability of role models, attendance at church, exposure to games and activities, moral teaching in the home, setting an example of maturity and responsibility, and so on. Every aspect of the environment provided will impact children to some extent. The environment is not some vague force but rather it is what we make it to be, and what our kids learn to make it be. The essence of being an American is to act—we are in control!

> **FATHERS MATTER!**
>
> "Families and societies fail in the absence of self-restraint. Fathers who instill it are in a very real sense the trustees of civilization, and they hold its future in their hands."
>
> Reuven Bar-Levav, M.D., *Every family Needs a CEO*

Today's successful democracies followed in the footsteps of the few successful countries in history. They were all built by enterprising people who fashioned an empowering framework of institutions, beliefs, and practices that supported their positive attitude toward life. They shaped their cultures to accommodate what they wanted. And when parts of the culture weren't working quite right, people like Moses, Jesus Christ, Martin Luther, George Washington, and Martin Luther King stood tall and made changes!

However, America is so large, and its people, and its regions, have grown so diverse, that there is no longer much uniformity about our culture. There are places within America where one is fortunate to be born, and there are places where it is quite unfortunate to be born. A child born into a safe suburban community or a wholesome rural farm community may be well considered luckier than one born into an inner city slum. A child born anywhere into a two parent household will on average have an advantage in life over one without such nurturing and guidance. It requires a very strong genetic nature to overcome a negative environment, and conversely, a strong environment can do wonders for even an average-to-poor set of genes.

During America's earliest years, the family environment played a larger role than the outside environment, and the guidance and nurturing of a good family was instrumental in giving children a head-start in life. During the last fifty years, the American family has diminished in importance, and the *nurturing* it used to provide has been lost for many of our youth. Not only is there a decline in two parent families, but the rapidity of the decline is astonishing: In 2012, only 66 percent of American households were family households, down from 81 percent in 1970. Between 1970 and 2012, the share of households that were married couples with children under eighteen halved from 40 percent to 20 percent.

In the same period, one-person households increased from 17 percent to 27 percent. One-third of American children, a total of fifteen million kids, are now being raised without a father. Nearly five million more children live without a mother. That's a total of 20 million children being raised without either a mom or dad. The majority of black children nationwide-54 percent-are being raised by single mothers. Among black families below the poverty line, 88 percent have only one parent present, which is, perhaps, a main reason why they are there.

The 20 million kids in single parent homes will grow up without some of the capabilities they might have developed with two parents to guide and direct them, and as a result, many of them will be severely handicapped compared to those raised in better environments. This unfortunate trend is one of the forces increasing the inequality of the American people, the numbers keep getting worse, and no one is doing anything to reverse this destructive path we are on.

It has been established that kids whose fathers are present as active parents in early and middle childhood have fewer behavior problems and higher intellectual abilities as they mature. And yet, in 88 percent of all black families below the poverty line, the children are being raised without a father present. They are subsisting primarily on government welfare of one form or another. And it is probably true that most of them are held back by both an unhealthy environment and the genetic legacy from their parents. Their only hope is that either they have a super mom or they get into a nourishing pre-school program followed by a good public or charter school. But very few of them have been encouraged to even want to follow such a positive path.

The fact is that America's culture, after a couple hundred years of success, has gradually changed in the past century. The depressing figures given above on our growing income inequality, the increase in illegitimate births, the violence of gangs in cities, and the decline in the percentage of people working, have all come about from changes made during the recent past.

Those changes cannot be blamed on Big Oil, or the drug companies, or capitalism, or global warming. They have been the work of those who undermined the family, denigrated religion, rewarded bad behavior, stole from the public funds, distorted the economy, celebrated a hedonistic lifestyle, misused drugs, or advanced one too many taxes, regulations, and restrictions on those who work. If you examine each of those negative changes, it will become clear that none of them could have been the work of the common people-they all sprang from actions of the elite leadership of the country and that is why we need a change of leadership!

The American safety-net, designed to help those in great need, has been so extended that it subsidizes illegitimacy and fatherless homes and rewards their irresponsible fecundity with extra stipends. The War on Poverty has actually contributed to more poverty and in the process disintegrated the family as a bulwark of our democracy. The same people that have done that have also advocated easy immigration for all and citizenship to illegal aliens. All that while promoting readily available free abortions to empower our women and solve the growing population problem. Thus, they are increasing the population problem with one hand and reducing it with the other! Such is the folly of big government planners who think they can make things better! They are actually subsidizing in dysfunctional households an increase in population greater than the numbers of babies that they are killing! Those are the simple facts. They're not pretty, but we have to start telling it like it is!

If there is a lesson in all this, it is that when a culture supports positive values such as strong families and personal self-reliance, it is a mistake to make changes that sabotage those strengths. We know a couple things to be true: government agencies can never provide the necessary nurturing for our children that strong families provide; a home without both parents is not complete; and kids need nurturing from both parents.

For hundreds of years our founding culture produced self-reliant and self supporting individuals. Today, a growing proportion of our children are being born into negative environments and creating an expanding underclass of second-class citizens. Isn't it time we cut to the chase and try to figure out how to reverse this alarming course we are on? Handing out money has not and will not solve this problem. America has developed a nurturing problem and it will take sound thinking and strong management to fix it!

Chapter 9

FREE WILL AND ALL THAT

Almost three thousand years ago, when Homer wrote his epic tales about Troy and the struggles of the earliest Greeks, the importance of every individual was elevated to a natural right. The idea was new in the history of mankind, born in the days of Hesiod and heroic legends, when strong men and women forged their own destiny. Years later, a new term was coined for such self-motivated individual action: "Free Will" — the unique power of human beings to decide what they want and the motivation to fight to achieve their goals. The great myths describing the constant conflict between Greeks and their gods tell the original history of this struggle.

Naturally, the pagan gods usually won, but the idea that man could exert his own powers and talents to create his own personal destiny became a fixture of Western civilization. Because the obvious success of cultures embracing free will is so obvious throughout history, its acceptance has to be one of the great milestones of mankind. If we are to save our democracy we must keep that inspiring spirit of heroic action and free will alive in the hearts of Americans.

"We cannot change the cards we are dealt, just how we play the hand."

----Randy Pausch

Today's advances in neuroscience have enabled us to confirm, with biological evidence, the ancient notion of free will. Michael Gazzaniga recently published a book explaining just how the brain gives humans free choice on their actions. He opposes those "experts" who believe we are pre-determined to act in certain ways, to live our lives as bees and ants do, subject to the control of a selfish animal nature.

In *Who's In Charge?*, Gazzaniga explains how the brain works and reveals the complexity of its operation which is dazzling! It isn't just the brain at work, but its interaction with the rest of the body, most notably the endocrine system, and the hormonal system, and with the surrounding environment.[18] More dazzling still is that every human's biology is unique and varies widely, operating in very different ways for each person. This difference alone establishes how unequal we are.

Gazzaniga's main point however, isn't just to show the nature of the brain's almost infinite ways of operating, but to demonstrate that it does not operate in any pre-determined manner. Indeed, there are so many forces at work in our reasoning process that it is impossible to predict what action an individual might decide upon when called to act or speak.

There was a time, fifty to one hundred years ago, when the combined "deterministic" ideas of Darwin, Freud, and Einstein, ruled the scientific community. They admired the physical laws of the universe that established the fact that if proper measurements were made, all action could be precisely predicted. (Of course, any common sense view would have told us that people are different from rotating celestial bodies, and much more difficult to predict!) In any case, many experts writing books followed the lead of these intellectual greats and assumed we are just the product of our genetic make-up, and free will is a myth. Then along came quantum theory to explain why Newton's laws do not always operate—atoms do not obey the so-called universal laws of motion! Crazy stuff happens in the quantum world, and even crazier stuff in the human brain!

Gazzaniga writes of the complex systems that act in the human brain and the application of chaos theory to explain the inability to predict outcomes—or why a person acts as he or she does. A person is subject to so many sensory inputs, mostly un-measurable, and which act differently in each unique individual, that any reasonably accurate predictions of behavior are impossible. Then he goes back to consider what the brain is actually for—decision making. It gathers information from all sorts of sources to make decisions from moment to moment.[19] The only predictable thing is that the individual, using his or her own physical and mental apparatus, as conditioned by his or her experience and culture, will make a decision. We all make choices and some work out better than others.

Think of Tom Brady, getting set for the center to "hike" the football, scanning the other team's defensive line-up, reviewing his options, signaling to his players, and then executing. The team may have practiced a hundred play options, carefully plotted beforehand, but from moment to moment in the field, decisions have to be made. And even on those plays called in to him by the offensive coordinator, it was the coordinator who reviewed the situation on the field, and dreamed up the best play to use. There is nothing pre-determined about football!

And then, even if a play goes all wrong, Brady can improvise; he might slip by the rushing tacklers, and decide to run the ball himself, or lateral off to a team member to the side. Each play, even as it unfolds, calls for rapid decision-making and choices by the individuals involved. Each decision emerges from a brain that has calculated and evaluated innumerable real time observations and past bits of knowledge to decide on a course of action. That is free will at work! And, that is why all sane people are responsible for their actions.

Belief in free will is an essential to the rearing of children. If they are exposed to the idea that they are helpless pawns, they will not try; if they are not taught to be self-reliant, they will believe that they deserve help from others; and if they are conditioned to wait for others to act, to let someone else go first, they will hesitate and waste their talents. Since a democracy requires individuals to be involved and rational citizens, the attitudes of responsibility and self-reliance are its foundation stones, and a belief in free will is what empowers each individual to act in a constructive manner.

Some people are born with a lower sense of independence and self-reliance than others. For them, it is especially important that they be encouraged to act on their own behalf and not expect someone else to take care of them. A child that has not been shown the need to use his free will to accomplish constructive goals will have an unequal chance of success. Many parents fail in this regard by both their words and deeds. This waste of so many children's potential is a tragedy to not only the children but to the country. Destroying those virtues in people is the best way to destroy a democracy. Yet, that is exactly what the demagogues running for political office do every time they promise you something for nothing.

The importance of recognizing free will is that, not only does it exist, but accepting that premise is beneficial to everyone. The existence of free will is what underlies initiative, responsible behavior, integrity, and all the values that help communities of people work together. Democracy cannot exist without it. Get rid of free will, and there is no personal responsibility; no innocence or guilt, no premeditation of wrong-doing. Without free will, anyone, not just Flip Wilson, can just argue that: "The devil made me do it!"

Chapter 10

SURVIVAL OF THE FITTEST; PAST AND PRESENT

It has been believed until very recently that modern humans have remained substantially the same since they first appeared on earth about eighty to one hundred thousand years ago. That constancy of the entire human race was supported by the DNA analysis of all the current world populations and the fossil remains of our ancestors. The differences we see between the races were thought to be merely superficial things like skin color, body shape, hair texture, and height.

However, those findings were based on a study of the most obvious elements of our DNA. Recent studies have found that while the basic building blocks are very similar, there are large differences in the number of copies of the genes on each strand of DNA.[20] These new discoveries confirm that individuals are much more different than once believed and that there are significant differences between people of different regions and heritages.

What has happened is that humans have been subject to the simple laws of genetics, with parents passing on various personal traits, which are not clearly identified in our DNA. For example, individuals have varying degrees of disease resistance, initiative, patience, risk tolerance, persistence, and so on. Most of those factors had to play a role in who survived and who perished, not only thousands of years ago when we were faced with the uncontrolled natural environment of fang and tooth and claw but also subsequently when we had to survive in developing large societies.

After mankind tamed nature and lived in large social communities, different traits played a role, not so much in who survived, but who raised the most children to adulthood. The most successful at replacing themselves would have passed on their genes to those generations that followed. The skills needed for survival transitioned from those overcoming the physical environment to those that helped a person to succeed in complex societies. Those most successful usually had more children than the less successful, creating an ever-improving gene pool.

An interesting factor in this process of genetic improvement was the contribution made by the custom of monogamy. It is not clear why or how that started, but it must have been a deliberate creation of the people and their religious and political leaders. Based on what we know about genetics in the animal world, it is clear that chimps and most wild animals are herd animals, with the strongest and most aggressive males keeping a harem of females, thus passing on concentrated genetic traits of strength and aggression, but little else. Humans, by adopting monogamy, enhanced the reproductive success of *all* individuals, creating a varied population, with a wide range of genetic traits. Talk about taking different paths—chimps still live in small and unruly patriarchal tribes while humans go to symphonies, supermarkets, and the moon!

There are many people who have contributed greatly to our success who would not have survived a fully natural law of the jungle: people of passive temperaments, and small or weak stature but big creative minds. I argued in *Wasted Genius* that without monogamy, current Nobel laureates would look like a cross between an NFL quarterback and a sumo wrestler, and their prize categories would be limited to wrestling skills and the forward pass, not the esoteric scientific and technological discoveries that reinforced our growth out of the Stone Age. That positive impact of monogamy was enhanced by the deliberate *selection* of mates where the more competent individuals probably began to choose similar partners.

The combination of monogamy and mate selection must have accelerated advantageous changes in human competencies. There is also an elevated level of mate selection, called "methodical selection," where there is a very deliberate matching of parents specifically designed to pass on superior genes. Such careful breeding of superior specimens has been used to rapidly improve the characteristics of plants and animals, but few humans go to that extent to shape the nature of their children. Nevertheless, such a process illustrates the impact that any amount of mate selection can have in differentiating subsequent generations into different skill levels. The mating choices made, and the varying fertility rates experienced, must have created changes in all societies. If so, that process would have created some social groupings with either more or less capability than other groups. Imagine the progress that would come if such an even slightly above-average group of people also developed an empowering culture!

While all humans are on average very similar, there are those who have superior characteristics, and if a social group was made up with a disproportionate number of such people, they would have had a competitive advantage over other groups. In fact, such a concentration has existed in history and is well documented. Ashkenazi Jews, who followed a strict practice of intermarriage within their narrow racial and religious members, concentrated in their descendants a vastly superior cognitive capability in the scientific and mathematical subjects.

What happened, in brief, was a result of social conventions in Europe during the last couple hundred years. The great social gulf separating the lords from the peasants and shop-keepers decreed that the aristocracy could not muddy their hands with crass business matters. This custom created an opportunity for the Jewish community to dominate the growing financial businesses of Europe. Then, those individuals within the Jewish community who had the "quickest" minds in financial and mathematical matters, and possessed the persistence and resilience to operate such businesses, became wealthy. Finally, the most successful families inter-married, concentrating not just their wealth, but their superior mental skills, which improved with each succeeding generation.

The extraordinary result was that descendants of those people, representing a tiny fraction of the world's population, have garnered almost one-half of the Nobel Prizes in the hard-sciences during the last fifty years! Talk about inequality! When it comes to mathematical dexterity, comprehending bio-chemistry and quantum mechanics, while having a little extra persistence and tenacity, these individuals are light years ahead of the rest of us! However, the rest of us can take some comfort in the fact that more ordinary minds created the institutions and societies that allowed such a unique group to flourish. After all, no such thing happened in Africa, Asia, or New Guinea!

When it comes to science, the Ashkenazis are certainly a natural aristocracy. A similar confluence of talents, but in the field of political science, occurred in the American colonies in the mid-eighteenth century when a group of independent-minded individuals gathered in Philadelphia and declared that they had the right to liberty and would not bow to the king of England. Royalty and emperors around the world could no longer expect subservience from the people they ruled. These founding fathers of America formed a revolutionary culture of people that stood for liberty and self-reliance. It had been done before many times in history, but rarely so well or so long lasting. We can only assume that the genetic nature of the individuals involved— Adams, Franklin, Jefferson, Washington, and others, was a tad above the average! And it is fairly certain that their superiority lay as much in their fortitude, independence, and resilience as in their IQs.

Undoubtedly, there have been other times and places where similar unusual concentrations of abilities or lack thereof could have occurred and resulted in groups that were more or less than average in skills.[21] In summary, although our over-all DNA may have all remained the same, there are real differences in the abilities of different people and groups of people. Those differences come from all the positive traits that vary greatly between people but are not revealed by current DNA analysis.

The requirements for "survival" have changed over time and resulted in another form of inequality. Instead of killing lions with a spear, we have to balance our checkbooks, invent machinery, and sell our products and services. The advent of organized communities and advanced financial activities gave an entirely new shape to mankind's environment. Once alphabets were refined, and writing became commonplace, the race to the top began, and a whole new set of capabilities became critical to success. The environment affecting a society was its literacy, education, and social interactions. Hunting, gathering, even a lot of farming became mere hobbies of secondary importance.

Individuals were faced with the need to utilize new capabilities if they were to prosper in the more complex new communities. Those capabilities probably included such traits or tendencies as empathy, an ability to cooperate, arithmetic skill, persistence, and long-term planning. People with those traits fared well in the rapidly evolving societies and due to their success they were able to raise more babies than the less successful. Thus, while the definition of what was "fittest" changed, the process of survival of the fittest gradually narrowed to the survival of the most reproductive. Since successful and more affluent members of a community had the resources to raise more offspring to maturity than the less successful, the genetic composition of rapidly progressing societies would have been passed on by the successful people. Further research is needed to see whether such genetic improvement increased at an equal pace in those stagnant societies that could not expose their members to comparable escalating mental and social requirements.

A similar confluence of exceptional characters and a supportive culture could explain why the Industrial Revolution occurred so fully only in England. In *A Farewell to Alms*, Professor Clark suggests that the *downward* mobility of upper class values and genes in England created an unusual expansion of competent and motivated people in the middle classes. We may speculate, he writes "that England's advantage lay in the rapid cultural, and potentially also genetic, diffusion of the values of the economically successful throughout society in the years 1,200-1,800."[22] During that period, the wealthier people in England raised more than twice the number of children to maturity than the poor. He identifies the valuable traits passed on by the wealthy as thrift, hard work, prudence, literacy and emotional restraint—the same types of traits that Coach Wooden listed in his Pyramid of Success, the moral and positive traits that made his teams the best in the nation.

Note that in the quote above, Clark suggests that these enabling traits and characteristics that were passed down by the wealthy to a larger and larger portion of the population were both cultural and genetic. Modern neuroscience shows that many of those personality traits such as emotional restraint, thrift, and sound decision-making are by-products of one's unique biology and genetic make-up. The implication is that, as the wealthy out reproduced the poor, their children and grandchildren enlarged the proportion of the English population with both their middle-upper class cultural values and an advantageous set of genes. Certainly, if the successful people were out re-producing the unsuccessful by a factor of 2:1 for six hundred years there would have been substantial improvement in the nature of the population.

Professor Clark is careful to write that all races and people are equal, which is a necessary position if you are not to be attacked as a racist. However, he does seem to believe that the valuable traits, that make some people more successful than others, are not only taught to kids in good families, but are passed on in their genes. In an interview reported in Mother Jones, he puts it this way:

"Look at it this way: I'm five-foot-seven. No one is going to believe that I have any possibility of making it in the NBA. But for some reason, in these other aspects of life we somehow think that everything should be possible for people. I think maybe it's part of how we have to feel about the world in order to make our own way through it."[23]

Just as height is largely inherited, and impacts a person's potential, so are all those other important traits inherited. At birth, if you inherit a pre-disposition to more than average persistence, imagination, and initiative, you will do pretty well in life. If you also get the biological foundation for logical thinking, resilience, patience, and some EQ for people skills, you might become a great leader. If you get all that, as well as President Obama's great speaking ability, along with John Kennedy's hair, and Ronald Reagan's charm, you will certainly win the presidency!

PART III

CIVIL SOCIETIES - FALSE

STARTS & GOOD STARTS

Chapter 11

VOLUNTARY AND INVOLUNTARY MIGRATIONS

There are many statistics to prove America's success, but more convincing than numerical data is the fact that there has been a 400 year long one-way flood of people trying to move to America. The nation became a dream destination for millions of people soon after the first pioneers hacked out their homesteads along the Eastern seaboard. The arrivals all happily became "Americans" and worked to build a great nation. Because we know that it is the people of a nation that shape its destiny, we have to wonder what was so special about the Americans who built this best of all worlds?

For starters, we know that those people that migrated to Early America were almost exclusively Europeans that wanted freedom and opportunity. They came voluntarily,

willing to face the hardships of such a move. Those
Europeans that didn't come were probably not as enterprising or pro-active as those that dared face the wilderness on
these shores and rely on their own wits to survive. America
has been known for its "can-do" people, and that may be
because this was the type of people that came here. And
they came here in droves, wave after wave, for hundreds
of years.

If multiculturalists were right, historical emigration
trends would have shown equally large numbers of people
fleeing to Samoa, Tanzania, Peru, Bulgaria, Mongolia, even
the Arctic lands of the Inuits and Laplanders. But the vast
majority chose Western nations, and especially the United
States of America. That says a lot: Apparently all nations
and cultures are not equally attractive!

In a brilliant exposition of the road that lies ahead for
the American experiment, Thomas B. Carson describes the
American dream as "a term used to describe commonly-
held beliefs, assumptions and expectations of political freedom, economic opportunity, and material progress in the
U. S."[24] These are the three blessings that all immigrants
sought. They frequently arrived in America ragged and
poor in a financial sense, but with a wealth of initiative and
imagination. Once ashore, they ceased being "huddled"
masses and became Americans—individuals—their new
land's "ultimate resource." Carson's simple definition of

the American dream neatly summarizes the goals of these immigrants, as well as the goals that most of mankind has been seeking for several thousand years.

Humans have been on the move, relocating from one place to another, ever since first moving out of Africa. They went out and about, settling here and there, until every inhabitable area was occupied. Once settled, most planted roots, at least for a while, before moving on to another place. A few groups stayed put in isolated and sometimes unfavorable locales such as the Australian outback, the frigid Arctic, sub-Saharan Africa, or the wildernesses of North and South America. Some of the latter are still being discovered, living just as their Stone-Age ancestors had five thousand years ago, truly lost in time. Those inhospitable regions were the exceptions, their people denied a future of progress by their isolation, climate, geography, and their very bad choice of a homeland.

Most of the people that left Africa settled in more favorable areas, from East Asia and the central Asian steppes to the Middle East, Europe, and North Africa. Initially, they were hunter gatherers, but about ten thousand years ago some learned how to farm and raise animals. Then, strengthened by the security, calories, and comfort of farming communities, they enjoyed steady population growth, and began the long ascent to the present. By five thousand years ago, there were over a dozen large civilizations spread across the globe, each with governing institutions, some early forms of writing and record keeping, good food production, access to travel, trade, and communication opportunities, and all living in reasonably beneficent climates.

These people were however, constantly at war. Conflicts often took the form of massive invasions by hordes of fighting men, intent on conquest, looting, and adventure. But history often shows that disasters can create positive results from the new beginnings they force on people. One such creation was the city of Venice, founded by individuals who chose to seek a safe haven from the marauding invaders who attacked after Rome fell.

Northeastern Italy had been home to a group of industrious traders, living in prosperous cities along the Roman highways connecting Italy and the East. Their families had enjoyed the comforts of Pax Romana but that period was shattered in the third century when Rome's economy collapsed, destroyed by corruption, civil war, and foreign entanglements. The people of Veneto in Northern Italy were left helpless.

During the horrors of these barbarian invasions, some of the local inhabitants fled to the small islands tucked away in the marshy lagoons that lay along the Adriatic coast. Some of these people had fished there, and knew how to paddle small flat bottomed boats out to the remotest islands. That was where the more enterprising people of Veneto, loaded with whatever few possessions they could fit into their prams, fled to the safety and freedom of the lagoon.

Historian Thomas Madden asks "Who were these people...and why did they think it worth such unyielding effort?"[25] After all, it was not pleasant to move out and re-settle on small islands with poor soil, brackish water, and ferocious mosquitoes. Madden answers his question: "They chose merely to live free...and in those early years impor-tant elements of the Venetian character were forged. The Venetians were a determined people: determined to resist the changes that swept Europe, determined to remain loyal to their state and one another, determined to remain Catholic in communion with the people of Rome, and determined to fight the sea itself to achieve these goals."[26]

Those people who failed to move were left on the main-land, subject to the charity, if any, of the barbarians! What a difference is made by human action-or inaction! There have been many filtering situations in history, different paths taken, and it has made all the difference for so many people! Winners often vote with their feet, shaping their destiny by their own purposeful action.

The people who settled the islands in the lagoon went on to build one of the showplaces of modern man, and fashioned a republic that stood for a thousand years. They started early on, in 466AD, when the people elected three tribunes to act as their government. These democratic roots were built on the rustic conditions they endured. Poverty was equally shared, one kind of food sustained everyone, their homes were equally primitive, and there was no aristocracy. They produced salt from the sea and traded it for food and supplies and eventually became one of the wealthiest trading nations in the world. It is a story not unlike ours in America: Independent and self-reliant people voluntarily picked up stakes and moved to a harsh new land to preserve their freedom, creating a vibrant and successful new nation. The less adventuresome stayed put in France, England, Germany and the other nations of Europe.

Madden describes the founding generations of Venetians as "a collection of fiercely independent refugees, fused together by blood and cunning into one people."[27] They remained a closely knit society, constantly challenged by outsiders who threatened their freedom. Around 697, the Tribunes elected a chief executive to help oversee the growing nation. He was called a "doge," a single leader, the first of 118 doges to lead the republic. He did not replace the tribunes, but worked with them, his[28] power flowing directly from the people of Venice that he governed. The people retained the right to an assembly, which held the supreme power of government. Thus a republic was created by these people, a free form of government, *the only one left in the world*, and one that lasted a thousand years. And it was all built by a hardy group of voluntary migrants intent on establishing a free and empowering society of their own. Venice was not created by a government—it was created by a unified and determined group of independent individuals-just like America.

In recent years there have been similar mass movements into Israel that also illustrate how valuable some immigrants can be. When the Cold War ended in the late 1980s, Russian authorities could no longer stop the flood of people wanting to escape from the failed communist country. In the next ten years, about eight hundred thousand Jews moved from Russia to Israel, increasing the country's population by about 20 percent. This was a major blow to Russia and a boon to Israel. Although Jews had made up only 2 percent of Russia's population, they had represented about 25 percent of its doctors, engineers, and other professional classes. Those were "good" immigrants to get—competent, educated, and culturally similar to the nation they moved to. Of course, it is doubtful Israel would have allowed incompetent, illiterate, or culturally divisive people to enter their homeland! Only foolish ideologues would do that.

However, Israel is not without its problems. There is a large population of two minority groups who are quite different from the mainstream: the Orthodox Jews and Israeli Arabs. In those two minority groups, about three-quarters of the working age members are unemployed. With the mainstream Jewish civilians it's the opposite-about 80 percent are employed. This problem is exacerbated by the fact that a higher birth rate for the two minority groups is projected to increase their percentage of the nation's population from 29 percent to 39 percent in the next twelve years.[29]

This situation shows how immigration is good when it adds to a nation's workforce and social cohesion, but problematic when it creates major religious or cultural schisms. Thus, although all humans are on average, simply average, there are few societies composed of perfectly average people. "Averages" are just arithmetic calculations, and it is almost a certainty that some nations' people are above average and other nations' people are below average. One of the great Torch singers of Paris, perhaps Eartha Kitt, or Edith Piaf, was asked what she thought of French men and she replied, "Well, the brave ones all died in the war, the smart ones went to America, so we have what's left!" Her comment points to the fact that unusual circumstances, as well as sporadic voluntary migrations, can create large distortions in the composition of groups. Nations can never be equal, just the same as people and their cultures can never be equal.

Another example of voluntary migration's positive impact is the sudden flood of Englishmen into the North American colonies in the mid-seventeenth century. Within thirty years of the Mayflower's landing in Plymouth, with settlers eager to tame a cold and harsh wilderness, hundreds of settlements were established, land cleared, exports shipped, and farmsteads and homes constructed. Within a hundred years, the settlers had created a maritime industry equal to the great European powers. The people living in the world's one hundred poorest nations have not matched that rapid success at any point in history.

The American colonies had charters and constitutions, assemblies, and newspapers. The people were literate and self-sufficient. Yet, there were no public schools, minimal safety nets for the indigent, very small governments, and little or no regulation. But the people in the colonies thrived, and their children and grandchildren had built the world's greatest super-power in less than three hundred years when Woodrow Wilson took office as the twenty-eighth president of the United States a little over 100 years ago.

Those early Americans were all made up of voluntary immigrants who dared to take the long dangerous passage on small sailing vessels for months to get here. They knew that when they landed there would be very little comfort waiting, but rather, they would have to hack out a homestead from the forest, and start from scratch. These people who made the move were not an ordinary bunch of human beings. Many were Quakers, or Puritans, or later, members of the various Protestant sects, joined ultimately by Catholics and Jews, and a very limited number of other faiths. They were a self-selected group, for no one of less fortitude or self-reliance would have ventured on such a perilous migration.

Within 150 years these early settlers fought a war of rebellion and beat the super-power of the times— England— just because the king tried to regulate their shipping and tax their trade. These people were unusually tough and single-minded. They drove out the Royalists who thought we should negotiate with the king. Such weakness was not a part of the majority's mind-set. They tarred and feathered dissenters, and most Royalists learned to be quiet or move back to England or one of its other colonies. Thus, here again the American character was crystallized: those who would compromise left, leaving a more combative and determined populace to fight the war. And it was those who remained that built the world's greatest economy and military power.

While all people of all colors may be roughly equal, those who chose to settle Venice, move to Israel, or get to America were not—they possessed inordinate amounts of initiative, self-reliance, religious zeal, persistence, and resilience—the characteristics that make successful people and bolster their nations. IQ had little to do with it. Potential had nothing to do with it. These people arrived with axe in hand, determined to build a mighty nation, and they did!

Similar situations have been seen throughout history. Whenever a fiery and determined group of individuals wanted to escape the mental and physical oppression that marked almost every region in the world, they looked for remote undeveloped areas where the surrounding super-powers might not bother them. The Phoenicians settled on the rocky peninsulas and islands off the Eastern Mediterranean coast. Their freedom and commercial maritime success attracted like-minded people and they dominated the shipping trades in the Mediterranean for almost a thousand years.

> "A whole new class of intellectuals has arisen to supply a history geared to what people currently wish to believe, rather than to the actual record of the past."
>
> Thomas Sowell, *Race and Culture*

Their overflow settled Carthage, one of the earliest democracies in history.

The Dutch chose the lowlands on the edge of the English Channel, built dikes to hold back the sea, created new land, and resisted outside rule. In 1581, they declared their freedom from Spain, with a Declaration of Rights that reads like a rough draft of Jefferson's 1775 Declaration of Independence which was written almost two hundred years later.[30] The Nordic settlers who migrated to and built farms in Iceland wrote a constitution establishing their representative government in the ninth century. Several port cities and islands in Northern Europe did the same, forming the Hanseatic League. These were all cases of voluntary migrations and gatherings of people who chose to establish their own free homelands. They were not average, but self-selected for a free and independent lifestyle. And they all prospered.

The question is: why have all these past and present democracies been in Europe, but can only rarely be found anywhere else on the planet? The first notable example in history of a democratic government developed in ancient Greece over twenty-five hundred years ago. That model was copied eventually throughout Europe but never took root in the Middle East, Africa, or Asia. There must have been something in the culture and/or the genes of the European people that could explain this, but we just don't know. And there are very few seeking the answer. No one dares to challenge the new orthodoxy that all people and cultures are equal.

George Will pointed out the ridiculous extent to which this politically correct fetish has gone: "In 1991 Florida, in a fit of modern 'non-judgmentalism' and 'multiculturalism' and all that, enacted a statute requiring public schools to teach that no culture 'is intrinsically superior or inferior to another.'...This told Florida's immigrant communities something they knew to be preposterous—that they might as well have stayed in Cuba or Haiti or wherever."[31] You can't make this stuff up! How can the supposedly brightest people in America create so much dumb thinking? Cultures are not equal and too much "diversity" destroys them!

Two recent politically correct books on the subject, by Jared Diamond and Kenneth Pomerantz, attributed historical national outcomes to climate, geography, the presence of beasts of burden, or just plain good luck in finding coal fields. As indicated in chapter seven such theories may be politically correct but they are still wrong: Since the days of the Assyrians and the Egyptians, over four thousand years ago, there have been over a dozen great civilizations with good climates, natural resources, good geography, and beasts of burden—and only the West rose to pre-eminence. Climate and geography played virtually no role in the different outcomes of those civilizations.

All we know for sure is that certain social conditions have repeatedly provided the nourishing soil for free people and open economies to thrive. And one of those conditions is a preponderance of self-reliant individuals motivated to start anew and build a better home. The voluntary migration of such people into new locales created the success of such "start-up"[32] nations. An incidental benefit came from the fact that aristocrats and intellectuals did not join the original move to primitive conditions—they came later and critiqued what the common people had done!

Such population movements are not always helpful events. Fifteen hundred years ago, the masses of diverse people that had moved into the heart of the Roman Empire were a burden leading to the nation's collapse. In Germany this year, where a large number of Muslim refugees have recently been welcomed, the refugees, mostly young men of military age, are out on the street attacking and occasionally molesting the ladies of Cologne. It is fashionable today to worship diversity, but how does having a divisive racial or religious group help a nation? Diversity is only good if the diversity adds positive strengths. Successful teams require several types of talented players, but they don't need good *and* bad players.

If there is a lesson in this, it is that a nation must control its borders and monitor who gets in. Rome failed to do that, and sooner or later they became overrun by the barbarians!

America was fortunate with its immigrant groups in two ways: First, for over three hundred and fifty years, the immigrants coming in sought merely freedom and opportunity. They were not the type of people attracted by generous welfare and medical care, because there was no such thing at the time. Secondly, they almost all came from Europe and were culturally similar, with Judeo/Christian faiths, and the same attitudes about government, the law, and religion. Contrary to advocates of diversity, that homogeneity worked well. And just because that positive mix of past immigration flows was beneficial does not mean that future immigration will be the same.

The large flow of people from the Middle East into Europe has recently been in the news. The receiving nations such as France, Germany, Holland, and the Scandinavian countries have been very homogeneous for a thousand years, and very successful. It is not clear how the "diversity" gained from this influx of Muslims will strengthen these nations in any way. Even if we ignore the jihadists that may be sheltered within this movement, the divisive culture and beliefs could fracture the unity of these nations. Recent street violence in Cologne that witnessed mobs of immigrants molesting the women has raised doubts about letting these foreigners in—especially since most of them are single men of military age. The resident women are even now wondering if they have to dress more modestly to accommodate the new arrivals' religious beliefs. Ms Marisa Micallef, the former ambassador to America from Malta, has called for tighter immigration controls in an article entitled: "First they come for the women..." She believes that "We must vet refugee men not for being jihadists but also for having attitudes incompatible with our way of life in Europe."[33]

In fact, the immigration situation has changed. We are currently not faced with the task of building a new nation but of maintaining the great nation that our grandparents bequeathed us. Our job is to pass it on safely to our children. Instead of needing more people, we need fewer! And, if we do let more in, we should make sure they will add to our human capital and not be a negative factor. We need not be the policeman of the world, or the savior of the world. We have enough troubles already!

Now, some compassionate people may believe that it is gracious to extend charity to foreigners, but even if you want to do that, doesn't it make sense to choose who deserves such consideration. A rational policy would establish guidelines for who is allowed in and who isn't. As it is, we are being inundated by young Muslim men and unskilled families from Latin America. Meanwhile, competent professionals who seek a proper legal entry have to wait for years in line to get into America. The State Department cannot even keep track of the hundreds of thousands who have overstayed their visas! It is, in short, simply a management problem. All that's needed is to enforce existing law, screen all applicants, and admit only those who fit a well-designed standard based on national need.

Chapter 12

UTOPIAS AND DYSTOPIAS; DREAMS AND NIGHTMARES

L et's start by admitting one thing: It is totally unrealistic to hope for world peace, orderly nations, honest people, and equality for all. Those four optimistic visions of a brighter future have set many minds afire. But such hopes and dreams for radical change can turn to ashes of despair when they fail—which they always will! The fact is that you cannot create a perfect world unless you populate it with perfect people and there lies the problem.

Intellectuals, who adore abstract theories and grand plans, are especially prone to reach for utopian goals. Plato was among the first to paint such a rosy scenario, but even with that some scholars suggest his *Republic* is actually an attempt to reveal the flaws in all utopian dreams. The twentieth century displayed in stark reality the results of such fantastical dreams.[34] Pol Pot, and fellow intellectuals, educated in Paris at the best universities, killed 20 percent of their Cambodian countrymen in an effort to create a new perfected society. Pol Pot had been steeped at school in some of the more unfortunate elements of French intellectual thought—Rousseau's hatred for society, his romantic illusions about the simple rural life, and the so-called glory of the French revolution. [35]

Like Pol Pot, the Jacobins, Japanese, Nazis, and Communists, abandoned the moral tenets of virtually every religion to seek an abstraction based on pure reason, a failed reasoning whereby they killed twenty or thirty times the "mere" 1.5 million citizens that Pol Pot killed—and they also still failed to create anything other than death and destruction. The horrors inflicted by those ideologically driven leaders demonstrate the need to think twice about "change."

The disastrous results of those utopian experiments lend credence to a book's subtitle I have used: "How Common People Create Successful Societies and How Intellectuals Make Them Collapse." Ordinary people rarely pursue complex theories—they wisely prefer to rely on good management and practical decision-making. In political matters, concrete thinking always trumps abstract thinking!

As Robert Conquest has warned, it is essential to keep intellectuals away from the levers of power.[36]

Nicholas Rubashov, a fictional communist official, makes a similar critique against intellectual thinking in Arthur Koestler's 1941 classic novel. After years of service to the Communist Party in the USSR, Rubashov's loyalty to the cause finally wavered when he looked back over those forty years and it seemed like he had been running amuck--"the running amuck of pure reason. Perhaps it did not suit man to be completely freed from old bonds, from the steadying brakes of 'thou shalt not,' and allowed to tear along toward some abstract goal—perhaps reason was a defective compass."[37]

Rubashov was wakening to the realization that all the carnage of war in the twentieth century arose from the theories of abstract thinkers. They sought to perfect nations, and had the arrogance to believe that their ideas were so magnificent that attaining them justified any means. It is the same arrogance that leads most of them to denigrate fiscal prudence, religion, simple honesty, and Western civilization and its moral principles. Consider the case of one of America's thousands of radical die-hards: Gerda Lerner began her career in Central Europe as a communist but emigrated to America and "taught" history at the University of Wisconsin, where she defended the USSR's brutal brand of communism and continued her condemnation of Western democracies.

Lerner eventually was liberated from the need to defend the USSR in the late 1980s after it collapsed, but admitted in her book *Fireweed* that she could never give up her fanatical dreams. "Like all true believers, I believed as I did because I needed to believe in a utopian vision of the future... and I still need that belief, even if the particular vision I had embraced has turned to ashes."[38]

His dreams became our nightmares-Karl Marx

Most Americans will find Gerda's story hard to fathom. How can anyone's mind work in such a crazy way? But she reveals just how far some abstract thinkers will go to escape from what they see as the restrictive bounds of reality. It has been the Gerda Lerners of this world that made sane people suggest that "radical liberalism is a form of insanity!" But, however crazy it may seem, we must learn from it and deal with it accordingly! Ms Lerner's career raises a few major questions for all common sense people to ponder: why do our schools hire such ideological extremists, how can people who need to believe in something so strongly ridicule my religious beliefs, and how do we keep such intellectuals from tearing down our country?

Granted, it is useful to look for improvements in one's culture and institutions, but the degree of change should be measured in proportion to the need. America does not need "fundamental" change; what we need is simply to clean up the corruption, reduce the inequality, and avoid foreign entanglements. These needs require only some easily enacted reforms. Most of the social and economic advances that made the West supreme came from continual tinkering with existing mechanisms to make them work better. Today, that common sense and carefully measured approach is needed more than any "total transformation."

Sports metaphors are helpful and easily understood: If your team is in the cellar, last place, it needs perhaps a total transformation. But if it is at or near the top—like, say, the New England Patriots—only minor adjustments, carefully executed, are appropriate. Similarly, if your nation is one of the best in the world, it is foolhardy to make drastic changes. That would be like trading away Brady and Gronkowski for some unproven players! Such changes would not create a utopia—except for the rest of the NFL!

Every sports buff must admit that they could never design a "perfect" football team. It should be equally, if not more clear, that there could never be a perfect government. It is possible that because humans are not perfect, they couldn't exist in a perfect world; indeed, if you somehow created a perfect society, and populated it with humans, it would no longer be perfect! And there is the added problem that people are different, so what might be perfect for one, would never be perfect for another.

All parents know that their kids will fight and disagree and that a firm, almost dictatorial, hand is sometimes needed to maintain order. That is because human beings have always been a notoriously unruly, cantankerous, and difficult bunch. That is why most governments in history have been tyrannical—that was the only way in which leaders could maintain any semblance of order. That also explains why it was a mistake for the United States presidents to topple the dictators in the middle east. There has been nothing but chaos in Egypt, Libya, Syria, and Iraq, since we interfered and worked to overthrow those leaders. It takes a special group of people to make a democracy work. That is why there have been so few of them and also why they invariably fail when their unity and drive weaken.

We know that socialism and communism, which hold out the promise of total equality, cannot deliver such an ideal state. Even moderate socialism contains the seeds of its own failure. Human motivation and freedom seem to demand the competitive struggle that creates income inequality. The best you can hope for is to keep those disruptive forces to a minimum and fashion an economy that will provide growing prosperity for all. Past democracies failed eventually because they grew too big to manage, too opaque to be understood, too diverse to work in unity, with classes set against classes, and were bankrupted by internal corruption and foreign adventures. Unfortunately, such disruptive forces have grown in intensity in recent years right here at home and America is showing its age.

> **A Lesson From History:**
>
> Karl Marx - considered by many intellectuals to be the most important social, political, and economic philosopher of all time.
>
> But all applications of his ideas and theories have ended in failure.

Ironically, these disruptive changes in our culture have been sold to the voters as a move toward a utopia. The whole idea of redistribution, income equality, sexual freedom, a release from the rules of religion, recreational drugs, and a big motherly government, is to create a utopia. The apparent goal is to save us all from competition, make everyone equal, let freedom become license to do as you will, abolish personal responsibility, concede that everyone is a victim needing the government to solve his or her problems, and even to recognize that merely "feeling uncomfortable" becomes a curable assault! Those goals may look like a utopia to some people, but it wouldn't look good to the people who built this country.

America has clearly been transformed from a republic to a failing democracy and the recent transformation of its people has been in profoundly negative ways. Note that the transformation is not of America, but of Americans. If our culture is changing it is because the people have changed, and that is the change that will make us crash and burn as a nation. The path we are on is seen as an opportunity by the lazy, and as kindness by the well-meaning, but it is a growing burden for those paying the freight. In fact, it is just a variation of Orwell's and Huxley's future visions—many of us are trading our freedom for the financial support offered by a corrupt government.

Democracies function best in small homogeneous societies that are bonded together by similar beliefs and customs-such as in small start-up nations or the small Scandinavian nations. Larger more diverse democracies develop the problems of fractured interests where many groups become activists for their own specialized concerns to the detriment of the nation as a whole. They turn into populist democracies that spend and tolerate themselves to death. Between domestic problems within, and wars from without, large nations have found it difficult to overcome grid-lock and manage their national affairs in a rational manner. They get lost in ideological battles and neglect the rules of sound management.

Some concerned students of this dilemma in our government have proposed adjustments to solve current failings. Those who simply want to return to the good old days, when things were simpler, are ridiculed, because there really is no turning back the clock. Granted there were idyllic times, small farms, pastoral scenes, many holidays, and country merriment. But with populations ten to fifty times as big, an expanded industrial complex to provide for all the people, and pollution abounding, the best one can do is visit a national park for an afternoon to bask in the beauty of nature. The underlying problem is too many people. Huge populations, and their accompanying vast amounts of consumption, rule out any return to those halcyon days.

Other reformers have suggested a return to local communities, a restoration of small regions, with self-governing systems, largely free of central bureaucracies. With today's huge population this plan would require a major devolution from urban to rural areas. It could be beneficial, but it is really just a matter of re-emphasizing states' rights and reducing the authority of the central government. Anything would be worth a try, but our current system is in such deadlock that no real change is imaginable. At least not by the type of people we are sending to Washington!

Armchair theorists have come up with several possible scenarios to overcome all these problems. Aldous Huxley's

Brave New World shows us the ultimate solution of what could happen if we fail to make democracy work: an elite take control by biologically and psychologically controlling the masses in a system not unlike the anthill or beehive communities. George Orwell's *1984 also* shows us the control that can be managed by an elite that rules by terror and mass psychology, a step more brutal than, but based on, Stalin's communism of the mid-twentieth century. Unfortunately, both books are dystopias, which illustrate possible horrible outcomes. They are the opposite of the futile utopian proposals, and show that the alternatives to what stable democracies offer are usually worse.

The dystopian novels show that to totally overcome the irrationality and greed of humans you must destroy their humanity. In Orwell's book, the brute force of the police and the power of psychological controls, are combined by an elite to control the masses. In Huxley's book, he suggests a simpler solution—rather than control people by force and the imperfect technique of advertising—use genetic means to render people more manageable. Basically he suggests a way of giving everyone a form of lobotomy, and drugs, to create an ant-like hill of automatons to do the work needed to keep the nation working in an orderly manner. That way there would be no Solcheniskis or Sakarovs, no Sam Adams and no Rosa Parks, to rock the boat! And it would be cheaper and more effective than the welfare state.

These projections of a dystopic future were written more than half a century ago when these writers first foresaw the difficulty of running huge modern societies populated by huge and diverse populations. Today, these horrid possibilities have become more plausible than when they were written. Modern genetic science has created a new and more revolutionary scenario for the future. A *transhumanist* future has been spelled out by a host of writers and reads at first like science fiction until you realize how close we already are to the physical and biological manipulation of human beings.

It is certainly a blessing to give amputees the use of wondrous new artificial limbs, to restore sight with a miraculous lens, and to transplant hearts and kidneys. But the trans-humanists see a greater and expanded opportunity to perfect *all* humans with major enhancements including adjustments to even the brains that make us tick. To these thinkers, we are all the "weeds" that Margaret Sanger wanted to replace with more perfect specimens.

Modern medicine will sooner or later make such manipulation feasible. We have conquered nature to such a degree that we will be able to redesign our bodies and brains. Charles T. Rubin suggests that "the more one thinks about how much better we could do if we designed our own bodies, the more dissatisfied we are likely to be with the present model."[39] After all, manipulating nature has been mankind's forte since we emerged from the Stone Age. We can finally put evolution under our own control, not just to improve the natural environment, but to improve our own capabilities. The million dollar man is right around the corner!

But as Rubin observes, man's tendency to overreach can lead to disasters, much as Icarus's flight in ancient mythology ended with a bang. Such a post-human future could lead to all sorts of change, but in the process we, as humans would no longer be human. And the changes wrought would undoubtedly be helpful to only a few and extremely harmful for everyone else. Such medical manipulation is no more than another form of eugenics, and although dressed up to appear as beneficial to mankind, would result in just another example of a dystopian future.

Predictions of the future may be speculative, but they do show the need to avoid any increase in centralized authority. When overwhelming power is given to an elite, they will sooner or later be attracted to coercive schemes in order to hold onto their power. And, such policies will be supported by academics and intellectuals like Gerda Lerner who have an unquenchable "need for a belief in the possibility of human perfectibilty," even if they know it is something than can never be! Utopian dreams are not for logical minds. But that is how abstract thinkers' minds work and they are taking control of our schools, our culture, and many of our minds. We must not forget that their best dreams could become our worst nightmares.

We have already started on the slippery slope to such dictatorship. Our presidents have gradually assumed more and more power; they can direct the hundreds of federal agencies to do their bidding, punish opponents with the IRS, snoop on private matters with the NSA, and raid your homes for drug or terrorism activity. We are not moving in a good direction when executive orders from the White House can change immigration policy, send troops into wars, and print money like crazy.

In effect, our government is already controlled in a despotic manner. If they control the availability of medical treatment, they can determine who lives and who dies! A president can either tear down the nation or build it back up to greatness. The way to progress may be gained by just removing the passions of ideology from the political mix and relying simply on good management. We have a great country but all the politicians do is quibble over social issues. Why not just try to manage the government efficiently, fairly, without corruption and favoritism? That could eliminate most of the problems plaguing us today. The Constitution allows, even assumes, that such will be done within the bounds of constitutional law. All it requires is that the voters pick a proven administrator, an experienced practical mind, someone who can clean up the mess we have gotten into.

Chapter 13

THE ROLE OF RELIGION:
PAST, PRESENT, AND FUTURE

It has been said that man is a social being and most people agree with that. But such agreement is not so common when one says man is a spiritual being. In today's advanced countries, being well fed, contented, and educated in the mysteries of the natural world, some people see no need for religion. Many look down on it as just a crutch for the needy. Even our president sneered at those small-town common people who "cling to their guns and religion." Nevertheless, throughout the world, during all recorded history, almost all people have clung to some form of religious and spiritual belief.

The president's remarks occurred several years ago, and were aimed at those individuals in the Christian community who held their faith in high regard. Curiously, several years later, the same president was lending support to Muslim immigrants and admonishing the nation's people to show respect for *their* faith. This double standard reflects both the arrogance and the error so often seen in our leaders' thinking. On the one hand, they parrot the politically correct mantra that all cultures, religions, and people are equally praiseworthy; then, on the other hand, they support a foreign culture while undermining our own!

There is no doubt that religions have shaped, and continue to shape, the culture of every society on earth. And, clearly, religions differ—some have helped their followers more than others. Just as it is true for horses and people, some religions are better than others. All religions have some good points; it is in the amount of negative qualities where the differences between them arise. Western civilization avoided most of the harm done by religions when some individuals suggested that we should separate our faith from our secular government.

About one thousand years ago, Europeans became increasingly involved in studying the physical sciences, reaching back to the great Greek and Roman scientists who were among the first people to develop mathematics, astronomy, and physics. This study of the hard sciences, although opposed by some church authorities, blossomed over the next millennium in Europe. Similar attempts by people such as the Islamic Mutazalites and the Islamic philosopher Averroes were suppressed by the Islamic priests who sought to maintain their exclusive power in a theocratic government.[40] This schism—about separating the spiritual world from the secular world—made the difference in human progress: The West succeeded and the Muslim countries stagnated; their minds became closed; education and technology dissipated; the priests remained in full control.

That radically different trajectory can be partly explained by the fact that the Western church, the Catholic hierarchy in Rome, was more fractured than Islam. The Catholic Church had three tiers of authority: the Pope and his Bishops in Rome, then the priests in every district, and at the bottom, the monks who opted for lives of austerity and study in isolated monasteries. Following the general historical rule that progress usually seeps up from the bottom, the monks devoted themselves to a life of study, which led them into the physical sciences, and thence to the creation of universities.

The first research oriented universities in the world were founded in Western European cities around 1100, and those centers of free thought gradually developed the scientific way of thinking that made the West supreme. In the twelfth and thirteenth centuries most ordinary people had little opportunity for study, but the Dominican, Benedictine, and Franciscan friars were able to create this revolution that made

Europe the leading scientific and teaching center on earth. It didn't happen overnight because the European church opposed "free thinking" that might challenge their authority. But it didn't happen at all in the Middle East because the few universities there only taught the Koran!

The early European rebels who dared voice their opposition to the closed mentality of their church were frequently made to recant or be burned at the stake. But they could not be silenced forever. It was a lowly and stubborn German priest, Martin Luther, who single-handedly reformed the Catholic Church when he stood his ground in 1507. After that, Protestant faiths spread like wildfire through Northern Europe and opened up a Pandora's box of free thinking, scientific inquiry, and innovation that led to the Industrial Revolution.

Humble Franciscan monk taught in 13th century European universities-Duns Scotus

Luther's contribution was built on over three hundred years of similar protests from Europe's learned monk-scholars. The Franciscan Duns Scotus, an early advocate of Aristotle's scientific thinking, was teaching at the universities in Oxford, Paris and Cologne two hundred years before Luther. Other scholar-monks, such as Marsiglio of Padua and William of Ockham preceded Luther by two hundred years, teaching at several European universities, and they advocated the heretical ideas of representative government and the separation of faith from science and secular matters. These men were all members of the Christian Church and they created the opportunity for all men to take giant strides forward.

Historians have struggled to explain why this progress, and eventually the Industrial Revolution, happened in Northern Europe and nowhere else on earth. Most academics of today write revisionist tales to deny that it had anything to do with a superiority of European people or their culture. That is because academic success in a politically correct America requires that all people and cultures be considered equally praiseworthy.

Thus, America's elite thinkers, and most of academia, are advancing a new enforced orthodoxy, the same kind of closed mentality and censorship that Luther fought to overcome. It is ironic that today's liberal elite, who generally disparage Christianity, have adopted the same rigid and censorious mind-set that prevailed in fifteenth century Europe.

Christianity's positive gift to the West was that it advocated, as one of its central doctrines, the sacred value of each individual. Christ's many parables taught his followers the value of love, kindness, and forgiveness. Professor George F. Thomas has described Christian love as "not measured out according to the value of the person loved, as human love is; rather, God is the Creator and His love is creative of worth."⁴¹ This bountiful and perfect love, extended to all, had great appeal among Western men and women and removed ancient fears and banished frightful idols. Because of this appeal, people of many lands voluntarily accepted Christianity which was spread far and wide, not by invading armies, but by humble missionaries.

When Saint Patrick went to Ireland in the fifth century, he told them that God had created them in his image and loved them all as a father. The Christian faith would protect them, Patrick told the Irish, and would deliver their children from evil. In so doing he liberated them from the need to sacrifice their children on their crude stone altars to appease angry gods. After all, Christ had died for them and only asked for them to love each other. Here was a story that answered their deepest needs—it is our lives, not our deaths, that this God wants.⁴² Christianity in that way offered a rock-solid foundation, freed from fear, dedicated to human action—a new found confidence and independence on which a revitalized Western civilization could be built.

More than a thousand years after Saint Patrick converted the Irish, John Knox arrived in Scotland, preaching the new Protestant form of Christianity. His work would upset the rigid structure of Scottish society. He arrived there in 1559, preaching to all who would listen, and the Scots embraced it. They accepted its harsh rules because it promised direct access for every individual to a faith that bound each individual together in a united community. "God loveth us," John Knox wrote, "because we are His own handiwork."[43]

Like all Protestant faiths, this dedication to the Almighty served to subordinate any obedience to another authority, whether a King, rich nobles, or the powerful priests of the established churches. Armed with this superior allegiance, the Brits and Scots spent the next 150 years wresting power from the aristocracy and giving it to the common people. Freedom grew so much in England and Scotland that King George could rightly complain, when his American colonies demanded total freedom, that they already were the freest people on earth and needed no more liberty.

But the people of the British Isles in the seventeenth century desired total freedom. Those who wanted it most picked up stakes and migrated in hordes to the New World where they would have freedom of religion, a free political system, and no oppressive aristocracy to hold them back. The cultural transformation that accelerated freedom of thought had been fueled by the Christian people of Europe who wanted to forge ahead in freedom, science, and political reform. That change in culture, exalting freedom and material progress, didn't happen anywhere else on earth.

It is a curious and ironic fact that some of the greatest technical innovations in history did not occur in Europe, but only gained general use there. Gun powder, paper, Arab numerals, and the printing press were the product of Oriental minds, but were only perfected and used in the West. The great empires of the Orient had scholar-scientists but they worked only for the elite in the Imperial palaces. Their output was vast but restricted to compilations and summaries of past works, rarely fresh or exploratory. It was the kind of erudition that Richard Feynman called "the disease of the intellectual" when he spoke of Islamic scholars who wrote not only commentaries, but commentaries on commentaries. "They described what each other wrote about each other. They just kept writing these commentaries."[44]

One of the greatest Islamic scholars, Ibn Sina, aka Avicenna, was considered to be the smartest man in the world, a man who knew everything, having memorized every book written by his eighteenth birthday.[45] But his knowledge was all about the past, not the future or the quest for new knowledge. Such scholars were invited to the Imperial palaces as showpieces, but never encouraged to learn something new. The autocrats and theocrats of Asia liked everything the way it was; they had no need to employ new technologies, and those beneath them had no freedom to. The cultures and religions of Asia oppressed the minds of their subjects, denying them any chance to explore new ideas or technologies.

The biggest problem with today's infatuation with multiculturalism is that it covers up how the other major religions of the world have in practice held their people back.

Mohammed led a conquest of many lands, and he imposed a tribal value system, a blood brotherhood, and a search for tribal honor—not a message of love and forgiveness. His troops invaded country after country, looting their peoples' possessions, and suppressing their liberty.

Followers of Islam were taught to meekly accept fate, banish pride, and accept one's total dependence on Allah. This set of beliefs was inimical to free enterprise, free inquiry, individual initiative, and technological innovation.

> "**Western civilization**, it seems to me, stands by two great heritages. One is the scientific spirit of adventure. . . humility of the intellect. The other great heritage is Christian ethics. . . humility of the spirit. These two heritages are logically, thoroughly consistent.
>
> ----Richard Feynman

And their rulers have for over a thousand years prevented any reformers from being heard.

One of Islam's greatest scholars, Averroes, who advocated scientific inquiry and the separation of reason and religion, was stoned in the Great Mosque of Cordoba and exiled from the seats of learning. He could have been the Martin Luther of Islam but his ideas were never allowed to take root in the arid soil of the Middle East. The theocratic state and its doctrine of submission to Allah had closed the minds and aspirations of its people.

Islam has proved for the past thousand years to be quite different in its impact than Christianity. It is really a governing institution as much as a religion for it dictates the lives of all its subjects—it is, in effect, just another type of dictatorship, but disguised as a religion. That is why that faith is incompatible with democracy and why its followers can never support democratic systems. It also explains why any attempt to pacify the religious sects or nation-build in the Middle East is doomed to fail.

The problem is not just the radical groups in Islam. No follower of Islam can swear to support the American Constitution because they don't believe in free speech, the equality of women, or the free elections essential to representative government. Instead, they believe in Sharia law, cruel and unusual punishment, the suppression of women, polygamy and harems, and dictatorial rule by the priesthood.

Similarly, Confucius, Buddha, and Mahavira held back their societies by emphasizing order and obedience over dissent and new ideas. The Chinese were on the verge of controlling the seas with a mighty navy in 1400 when Admiral Zheng He was ordered to return all ships to port. The navy's far reaching voyages were contrary to the rules stipulated in the dynastic foundation documents laid down by the Hongwu Emperor and also violated longstanding Confucian principles. The voyages had been allowed until that time only because the Ming's eunuch elite had gained a temporary supremacy over the administration's scholarly bureaucrats. But with the backward-looking leadership restored, the navy was closed down and for the next five hundred years the minds of the Chinese people were closed to exploration and innovation.

Another measure of religions is revealed in their record of reform: how Christianity unleashed science to explore the physical world over eight hundred years ago, inspired Luther's reforms of five hundred years ago, worked to end the slave trade three hundred years ago, supported women's rights to vote one hundred years ago, and strengthened the resolve of Black leaders to end discrimination and Apartheid this past sixty years. Meanwhile, Islamic nations still allow the horrific atrocities of old, the established cultural practices of gross brutality: throat slitting and be-heading, the honor killing of one's daughter for flirting, female circumcision, suicide bombing of civilians, the female slavery implicit in polygamy and harems, execution by stoning for adultery, and the forced isolation, burkhas, and suppression of women into a third class of citizenship.

History demonstrates the folly of any claims that all cultures are equally praiseworthy, that all religions have played equally positive or negative roles in mankind's advance. Indeed, such claims are guilty of the most extreme simplification and generalization that ever disgraced rational thought! It's comparable to claiming that all NFL football teams are equal, that Baptists and White Supremacists must be equally respected, or that the Yankees are as solid a team as the Red Sox!

There are simple and obvious reasons why major historical progress over the past thousand years was created by the people living in Christian lands and not elsewhere. It was not just a coincidence! All it takes to see this is a compass, a fundamental criteria for evaluating different societies. Armed with the Radzewicz Rule, the task is simplified: one needs to ask only which religious beliefs freed and empowered the most people, which beliefs gave them the support, the faith, and the encouragement to act. Conversely, religious precepts may be deemed to have been harmfully oppressive when they held back their people, discouraged active involvement, and stifled dissent and experiment.

Ironically, the American culture that was built by Christians and Jews, and invigorated by the Great Awakening, has seen its most educated elites distance themselves from religion. Many of our intellectuals have led the effort to repudiate our religious heritage. They find no use for it themselves and fail to understand why others need it, enjoy it, and depend on it. In doing so they distance themselves from both the altruism and love that most people find in themselves and the useful brake that comes from the inner voice of conscience.

Their atheistic position was well described by Koestler in *Darkness at Noon*, when the loyal Communist functionary lectured Rubashov, his wayward underling: "One may not regard the world as a sort of metaphysical brothel for emotions. That is the first commandment for us. Sympathy, conscience, disgust, despair, repentance, and atonement are for us repellant debauchery...God is an anachronism... When the accursed inner voice speaks to you, hold your hands over your ears."[46] That inner voice referred to comes from man's ennobling conscience, a moral brake that seems to be a genetic inheritance, a part of how human beings are wired, that must have played a contributory role in survival as people became more civilized over the last ten to twenty thousand years. It is no coincidence that the world wars and genocides of the twentieth century were perpetrated by autocratic governments that had abandoned the moral guidelines of religion.

There is recent scientific evidence that altruism is an inborn genetic trait that has been reinforced in many people through the forces of natural selection. In large cooperative societies, the mutual advantages gained from empathy and altruism are believed to have given a competitive advantage to those possessing such virtues. That is why even Rubashov's jailor, a godless Communist, knew of the "inner voice" that even he had to overcome in order to maintain his faith in the atheistic communist dictatorship.

In short, man has felt from time immemorial a deep need for spiritual support and religion has provided that for

many. It may be less important today for the more affluent and sophisticated. They enjoy almost total control over
their successful lives and property, so they believe they
don't need a religion. But they do not give credit to the
fact that most of the safety and wealth that they enjoy was
built by religious people living lives in accordance with the
teachings of the Jewish and Christian Faiths.

The only people willing to face the steel and hangman
of the aristocracies to demand their rights were those with
the passion and strength provided by their faith. It was the
Puritans in England in the seventeenth century that forced
many of the reforms that helped free the people. It was
only an unshakeable faith, strong enough to banish any fear
of the gallows, that allowed their struggle for freedom.
Centuries later, Bishop Tutu in South Africa never went out
to march in protest of the brutal apartheid regime without
his Bible in hand and wearing his Hassock. The Reverend
Martin Luther King, Jr. was a Baptist minister and relied
on the Christian message of love and respect for life to fight
discrimination in America. America's present freedom and
prosperity didn't just happen. It was built by the many
generations that preceded us and they were informed and
motivated by the Judeo-Christian culture that had helped
make Europeans the most successful people in the world.
It is a part of our culture that Americans cannot afford to
lose.

Chapter 14

WHAT MAKES A SOCIETY SUCCESSFUL? THE RADZEWICZ RULE REVISITED

When a coach reviews the last game tape with his players they all become historians. They are searching for the good things they did, to continue them, and for the mistakes they made, in order to eliminate them in the future. They like winning, so they fully understand the old saying that "If you don't know history you will keep making the same mistakes over and over again." But you don't just learn from avoiding past errors-it's also good to know what worked well so you can repeat those things! The best way to know what works in governmental affairs, and what doesn't work, is to look at history, for just about everything has been tried before. It's amazing what you can see if you just look!

In government, our leaders fail to understand such simple logic-they throw out many of the practices that worked in the past and create new policies that have always failed in the past. A wise man once said that repeating past mistakes is a form of insanity, and that may be the best description of what's going on in Washington today. All they have to do is look back over human history to see what caused mankind's historic advances and what caused its major misfortunes. Understanding those lessons of history is important for everyone: if you don't know what actually created our current well-being, you might join with and help those who are undermining it.

Most people think that historic advances were made by great military leaders, philosophers, political elites, famous diplomats, the aristocracies and royal families, or the people with the highest IQs. Ironically, those were the historic figures who got everyone into wars, wrote huge books explaining what people had already done, and laid claim to crippling taxes from all the ordinary working people. When it came to actually building or creating a useful tool or system, those were the people who went missing. That is why we must give credit to all the common people who are in fact their societies most valuable resource.

The first requirement for material and social progress has always been provided by the militias, soldiers, and sailors who provided a safe homeland. Then, with a secure environment, social and economic advances could be fashioned by the merchants, mechanics, lawyers, farmers, and workmen who made everything happen. But they could only make things happen when they were free and motivated to do so. In most of the world since time began, the people were enslaved in physical and mental bondage. In places and times where that was the case, little progress was ever made, even if people were physically safe. History shows that progress and wide-spread prosperity emerged only when a combination of security and freedom gave people the opportunity for positive human action. But history's emperors, kings, and sultans almost always stamped out such islands of freedom in order to keep a tight grip on their subjects.

The scholars and academics who write our histories will rarely give credit to the common people of a society. They prefer to dwell on the generals who led millions of soldiers to their death, or imperial courts where the elite lived in opulent splendor, or men of intellect wrote monumental books, or dictators ruled flamboyantly for better or worse over their subjects. These historians admire the palaces of emperors, their fancy china and linens, and mistakenly judge past societies by such opulence rather than whether the average person's well-being was advanced.

This bias in our history books occurs because these scholars and academics identify themselves with the elites and intellectuals of those periods and not with the common herd who supported the luxuries of their rulers. But it has generally been true that innovations, new businesses, and creative institutional systems all came from the bottom, from the working and managerial class, and flowed up and were widely adopted if they worked well, but abandoned if they didn't. The great historian, P. T. Bauer, documented this flow of innovations from the bottom when he challenged the "prevailing notions" of established economists and academics and, instead, credited the "individual voluntary responses of millions of people"[47] for mankind's progress.

The Radzewicz Rule:

$$S + EF - O = P \& H$$

A nation's most valuable resource is its people because they are the driving force behind innovation, production, and investment. Nothing happens in a country without the action of its people. Because those achievements arise from the contribution of all the people working, the process can be described as a team effort. Each nation is built by the team effort of its people. And to use a sports analogy, the nation with the best team will be the most productive and affluent nation in the world. Just as in sports, the winning team is the one with the best players, especially if they are organized by the best coaches and possess the cohesiveness and attitude that makes them unified. The history of nations shows that the winners possessed such assets.

If you examine the few nations of the past that succeeded in providing a good homeland for their people, it is very obvious what worked. It is so clear that it can be reduced to a simple equation, the Radzewicz Rule,[48] which shows what has always been required for a nation to succeed economically and provide its people with the pleasure of improving their financial lot in life and pursuing the happiness that Jefferson decreed as a right of all free people.

The symbols in that equation tell us that Safety plus Economic Freedom minus Oppression equals Prosperity and Happiness. If you have ever played board games, such as Risk, you may understand the need for security and safety for a society to prosper. In that game, you quickly learn that it is foolish to try and hold Poland among your territories, because it is surrounded by vast regions that will attack you from every side. If you read Michener's book, *Poland*,[49] you will see that in actual history that exposed location subjected Poland to continual invasion from all sides. It was much better to try and control isolated areas with few borders where invaders would find it more difficult to attack—places like the British Isles, South America, Southeast Asia, the Venetian swamps in former days, the ancient Phoenician islands and peninsulas, or even, as our ancestors found out, North America.

In actual history, England had that great advantage of being a fortress island, never invaded after the Norman Conquest in the thirteenth century. This gave them the stability and security evidenced by the neat farms, with stone walls and hedges, used profitably to farm and raise livestock for centuries without violence or destruction. In more recent centuries, the innovative residents were free to exploit their technological ideas to improve the production and marketing of products. Compare this to the turmoil in tribal regions where neighboring communities constantly attack, burn, loot, and enslave their neighbors. Such constantly fighting tribal groups never get a chance to build anything!

The English people also created the advantage of having secure property rights, deeds, and financial institutions that allowed them to operate their business in a safe and ordered manner. This was a cultural advantage, fought for by the common people, and it did take about eight hundred years to be fully gained, but it was gradually achieved, and provided the institutional foundation to secure the safety and transferability of each individual's property. Thus, the S in the formula requires both the personal physical safety of the citizen and also the safety of his or her private property. A primary weakness of all socialist and communist systems is the absence of personal property protection. People will just not work very hard if they can't keep the fruit of their toil. That's how human minds work and all communities have to deal with it! It's also why socialism and communism fail.

The EF in the formula refers to the need for an open and relatively free market place that allows each person to earn a living for his or her family and to save and invest any extra income. A democratic vote is not actually needed if *economic freedom* is maintained because a people who can support themselves and their families enjoy freedom and have the independence created by their earnings. People can have the vote, and still not be free if their ability to earn a good living is negated by taxes, rules, corruption, and regulations.

Perhaps the most frequent feature of dysfunctional governments is the Oppression of the common people. Successful societies do not have authoritarian rulers who exert oppressive demands on their people. And successful nations also do not allow the minds of their citizens to be oppressed by philosophies, religions, political correctness, and cultural obstacles that diminish their liberty. Oppression can be both physical and mental.

Most people in most countries have, throughout recorded history, been sorely oppressed and enslaved. The chains came from both arbitrary rulers and from some of history's theological and philosophical beliefs. The latter have often discouraged or even prevented their adherents from being innovative or rebellious. Most of the Eastern religions, and certainly Islam, have held back human progress because their belief systems discourage independent human action and thought. A democracy will probably never survive under Islam because the very nature of a theocratic state is incompatible with the principles of liberty. Give presidents Bush and Obama credit of sorts—they proved by their failure that we can't build a democracy in the middle east!

> **Why Attitude Matters:**
>
> "Over and above their test scores, we repeatedly find that pessimists drop below their 'potential' and optimists exceed it."
>
> Martin Seligman, *Learned Optimism, How to Change Your Mind and Your Life*

When religious dogma controls science, education, the media, entertainment, and the government, there can be no free thought or action. It can truly be said that the separation of church and state was "the secret weapon" of the West that allowed it to become the most successful civilization in history.

In *Common Genius*, the Radzewicz Rule is explained and lists those few instances in history where people gained financial and political success, and also explains why other nations stagnated. But admittedly, there is still a missing ingredient—some intangible that made some people more pro-active, more resilient, more persistent, and more ambitious than others. This is a necessary caveat because there have been some instances where there was an ordered and secure society, with an open economy, that did not put it all together and prosperity was never available except to the elites.

The missing ingredient could be the nature of the people. Most of the innovators, who created the hundreds of mechanical and electrical machines that powered the Industrial Revolution, came from the families of ordinary craftsmen. There may have been a genetic element to explain why such a flood of ordinary rural farm boys, apprenticed out to the trades at young ages, were the ones that most frequently became the builders of the modern machine age. Or perhaps credit should go to the custom of getting those children's brains actively involved in constructive pursuits while they were still in their teens, when their myelin developed best. Or it could be that the Protestant religion and its Puritanical culture put such an emphasis on work and achievement that it brought out the best in its followers. In brief, there may have been a boost from both a genetic advantage and a cultural stimulus. The Protestant Reformation represented an extraordinary cultural change that unleashed in its followers both a passion for work and newly opened minds eager to explore every facet of their world. After Martin Luther's brave stand, in the 1,500s, many of the repressive elements of oppression were finally vanquished in the minds of the people of Northern Europe.

Although, there are still questions to be answered, the Radzewicz Rule does explain the basics of what makes a successful society. And, it indicates what makes a country unsuccessful: If you have a nation where corruption and gross income inequality has tilted the playing field, those two evils of *economic freedom* will be destructive to the nation and its people. If you have a nation where you must parrot politically correct notions, that oppressive orthodoxy must be banished, because it closes the minds of those afflicted to new ideas and logical thinking. If you live in a nation that lets you vote, but taxes half your income, you are not economically free and certainly not happy. And you know you're in trouble when the president appoints the biggest Wall Street bankers to run the Treasury and the Justice Departments, and then looks the other way when they manipulate the economy and financial regulations for their own benefit.

Unfortunately, those evils, all contrary to what the Radzewicz Rule requires, are painfully present in America today. And they are crippling her. Income inequality is getting worse. Schools are getting worse. Class divisions are wider than ever. And, Congress is not about to change it. Our situation is the reverse of the Radzewicz Rule. We now have S-EF + O = S&U, which reads, Safety minus Economic Freedom plus Oppression equals Stagnation and Unhappiness!

America is still the world's super power, with a high standard of living, and a more affluent population than other countries, but that pre-eminence was created by prior generations and they were inspired by our original culture. Today's people, even the parents of today's Americans, did not build America. It took centuries to build a nation such as ours, and it was built by different people and was based on a culture quite different from today's culture. We are living off the momentum gained by our grandparents' efforts but even that force is running out of steam.

Just as prior democracies got too big, too diverse, too corrupt, and burdened by a government too big and too opaque, we have done the same, and are going downhill. While Americans argue about social issues, and allow illegal immigrants and refugees to flood the nation, the rest of the world is moving ahead. Several nations are planning to replace the use of the dollar as the major international currency, our national debt has soared to $18 trillion, our soldiers are dying in foreign lands in wars we can't win, in places we don't belong, deficits continue to pile up more debt, our financial system continues to enrich the few while the bankers risk our deposits with speculative practices, and the leaders in Washington are deadlocked over partisan battles.

There are very few candidates for political office that have the ability to change the direction we are headed.

The current trends that reveal our downward trajectory have been in place for too long to be easily reversed. Voters think we need a dignified presidential figurehead for that office, the type that is cautious in his speech, careful to avoid politically incorrect gaffes, balancing all sides of an issue to antagonize no one, and reluctant to try harsh remedies. But, that has not worked. Nothing much has worked since Reagan and the Pope got the Berlin wall torn down.

What we need is a very firm leader like Lee Kuan Yew who made Singapore an economic powerhouse. Such a brash tough individual could speak the truth, level the playing fields, clean up the Wall Street banks, let the chips fall where they may, and bring a businesslike approach to the national leadership. Kuan Yew ignored ideology and theories, made pragmatic common sense decisions, and insisted on honesty and good behavior from everyone. Is there any better way to run a country?

PART IV
TODAY'S PROBLEMS;
THE FRIENDS AND ENEMIES
OF DEMOCRACY

Chapter 15

THE AGE OF THE EXPERTS, INTELLECTUALS,
SAT TESTS, AND ABSTRACT THINKING

There is no need to try and prove that experts can be bought, or that they are willing and able to prove just about anything one might want to prove. It is common knowledge that their studies, focus groups, surveys, and computer models are both flexible and unreliable. Recall the engineers who proved that, under the laws of aerodynamics, bumblebees cannot fly! These types of commonly incorrect mental gymnastics are a recent curse in America and result from the elevation of abstract thinkers over concrete thinkers. Any person scoring extremely high on SAT tests may be considered dangerous for his or her tendency to indulge in such fanciful theorizing. There are too few among those types who manage to keep their feet on the ground.

The mental confusion implicit in abstract thinking also explains why the recent administrations in Washington can simultaneously criticize Christianity while defending Islam; protect and support middle eastern oil production

Fought Apartheid armed with only his bible and hassock-Desmond Tutu

while blocking American pipelines; and while condemning the so-called 1%, appoint its most corrupt leaders from Wall Street to run the Treasury Department and Federal Reserve Bank. Our great nation, which has always been known for common sense and practical wisdom, has somehow been taken over by the most brilliant egg-heads in the world––and they are killing us!

At the end of November, 2015, President Obama went to Paris for a meeting of world leaders to discuss environmental issues. In his formal speech, he told the assembled foreign leaders that fighting global warming would defeat terrorism and the related slaughter of innocents by suicide bombers. This occurred shortly after all of France had been shocked by a mass slaughter in Paris by fanatic Islamic madmen wielding automatic weapons, praising their god Allah, and shooting everyone they saw inside and then escaping.

The president's speech was followed by scattered polite applause but everyone wondered how there was any connection between the climate and Islamic terrorists. After all, dozens of radical religious cults within Islam had been assassinating infidels and each other ever since Muhammad founded the faith almost 1,500 years ago—and that was 1,300 years before the internal combustion engine and power plants had been invented.

President Obama's speech to the still-grieving Parisians is a vivid example of the disconnect between reality and the thinking of many of America's elite leaders. One of the unfortunate results of our schools' veneration of SAT scores and school grades is that children who can think abstractly have been advanced to leading schools and then on to leading positions in our nation. This is another situation where changing cultural attitudes have created a division of people into abnormal groupings, a process that creates inequality of opportunity and inequality of results.

> "**Ideology** serves as a proxy religion for people who view themselves as too smart for traditional religion. And since worshipping a god is an impossible task for the self-obsessed, the intellectual moron worships himself-man-and the ideas that will deliver us all into salvation."
>
> Daniel J. Flynn

Much of the public has come to actually believe that those with high IQs are more important to the country than those with lower scores! The result is that people with high grades get favored treatment in our schools, and those who think more concretely get neglected.

This process has also shifted power and influence to those who pursue ideologies that are based primarily on a beautiful vision or concept but which may have little practical use or likelihood of success. In fact, the pursuit of ideologies by abstract thinkers has created most of our problems. What we need is less ideology and more common sense and logical businesslike management.

Thomas Sowell has explained that this cultural shift into opposing groups arose because of the different way minds work. In *A Conflict of Vision*, he explains how abstract thinkers' minds see things differently from concrete thinkers. The former thinks in theoretical ways, favoring elaborate concepts and theories. They are entranced by utopian dreams even though they can never work. The less intellectual people follow a practical and mechanical process of adjusting their ideas to real world applications and testing how they work, then making small adjustments to make them work better. The difference is that concrete thinkers' mistakes are smaller and get corrected, while abstract thinkers' mistakes can be catastrophic and remain in effect, uncorrected, doing unintended mischief for years!

An example of the harm done from this faulty vision was the seventy years that most Western intellectuals remained sympathetic and even supportive of Russian

Communism. Seventy-years encompasses a couple generations of people who fell for Lenin and Stalin's utopian claims about gaining total equality under the Soviet system. Of course, within fifteen years of the revolution in Russia, millions of peasants had died as a result of the government's forced relocation of farmers' families and the collectivist policies under Stalin. And, during those days, the 1920s and 1930s, the American media had already begun its biased reporting supporting radical socialist theories: The New York Times reporter, Walter Duranty, won a Pulitzer Prize for reporting how wonderful Stalin's programs were working. His memorable excuse for Stalin's crimes, "You can't make an omelet without breaking eggs," has served ever since as an intellectual's validation of "the end justifies the means."[50]

In spite of the obvious failure and brutality of the system, abstract thinkers adored the idea of a society where all were equal, even if in fact, millions were sent to Siberian slave labor camps for opposing the scheme! Such is the failed way of thinking of the best and brightest, the people who prefer to pursue grand concepts rather than face reality. It is incredible that they ridiculed those people who held a faith in God, and yet joyously leapt into the arms of Josef Stalin with an unshakeable faith that communism would help mankind. And they clung to that faith-even after 50 years of demonstrated failure!

That type of radical thinking, common among the far Left liberals, has come to dominate our educational system. Instead of being taught the essentials for surviving and getting a job in today's world, the students are indoctrinated into a perverse hatred for our culture and its past. In an absurd desire to erase that past, schools are trying to rename Thanksgiving Day as the Fall Harvest Day, and Christmas as the Winter Holiday. They have already erased Columbus Day and presidents Lincoln's and Washington's birthdays! Stay tuned—July Fourth and Patriots' Day may be next!

Dr. Thomas Sowell has written about an important distinction that affects education—the "hard-sciences" versus the "soft-sciences." In the hard-sciences, dealing with inanimate physical objects, such as chemistry, engineering, and rocket-science, an abstract thinking mind can be helpful. It takes a sharp mind to understand astro-physics and quantum mechanics! However, it is safe to say that less than one tenth of one percent of college students can comprehend those subjects. Thus, there is a lot to value in A+ student—*provided* they go into the physical sciences.

However, those pursuing soft-sciences do not need the same level of IQ intelligence for their life work, and, in practice, bringing a highly flexible and abstract mind to many careers has done great harm. The "brilliant" but destructive shenanigans on Wall Street, packaging derivatives and bundles of sub-prime mortgages, is the most recent work of such clever characters. Goldman Sachs makes a point of hiring only the brightest graduates from the top Ivy League schools, because their minds are suited to trolling the shady edge of legalities as a way to make obscene and what should be illegal profits for their elite traders and speculators. We would be much better off if lesser minds, honest, responsible, and moral people, conducted our financial affairs. Apparently the people we elect do not want honest, responsible, and moral people in government—they wouldn't fit in!

Many soft-science "experts" attempt to claim in their own work the kind of certainty actually found in the physical sciences-such as the proven laws governing the circling planets and the laws of gravity. Such attempts to do the impossible have reduced the level of logic and common sense in our schools to new lows. Such soft-science experts are the ones who deny chaos theory and create computer models showing some horrid future if the trends in their data continue in certain assumed ways! How abstract can you get? Most of it is garbage in, garbage out. And if the computer doesn't confirm their preconceived theories they adjust their data input! For many, the sheer beauty of their ideas outranks their accuracy or practicality.

Our children are exposed to this twisted and anti-American propaganda in their schools and will either be disillusioned with their country, if they believe it, or fed up with schooling, if they question it. But, when a constant stream of people from all over the world strives to reach a single destination for four hundred years, even the dullest student should be able to connect the dots. But many do not, and go through life partially brainwashed to buy into the latest anti-America dogmas. And it makes you wonder: for many students, is today's schooling doing more harm than good?

John Podhoretz is a leading public intellectual whose record of ideological thinking reveals a lot about why intellectuals should not be listened to seriously, even though, admittedly, their verbal virtuosity and clever writing skills are admirable. In his book *Ex-Friends*, he recounts his radical youth as a member of the Far Left radicals in the 1960's when he supported almost every new extreme Left political position including general approval of Soviet Russia's policies. But, to his credit, he eventually lost faith in his fellow radicals and they became the ex-friends he exposed so vividly in his book. In an interview on CSPAN he was asked why it had taken him twenty-five years to see the light and switch from a pro-communist radical to an anti-communist conservative. He explained that, being an intellectual, it took him twenty-five years to see what any ordinary person with common sense would know immediately! Give him credit for that! And pray that after another twenty-five years he will swing to being a rational advocate somewhere between these extremes.

After his conversion, Podhoretz's political opinions veered sharply to the right and he became a leading voice for the Neo-Cons, the equally extreme right wing of the conservative movement. He contributed a bevy of articles to *Commentary* magazine, including a strong defense of the Iraq invasion, with the added suggestion that we should invade Syria while we were at it. Now, understand that *Commentary*, like *The National Review*, is run by the right wing intellectuals' answer to *The Nation*, the Left's most liberal magazine. All three are quite out of touch with Middle America, and proudly so, even if it means their total combined circulation is less than that of most metropolitan scandal sheets.

What is of interest here is how, in the run up to the 2016 elections, the *National Review* put out a hit piece against one of the Republican candidates with essays by some of the leading conservative intellectuals that that particular candidate was not a true "conservative." This was an example of the useless bickering over abstract principles that distinguishes intellectuals from ordinary Americans. And this divisive carping came from people who have been talking and writing for the last thirty years with no net impact on society. It is telling that the candidate's poll numbers increased after the attack ads. If there is a lesson here, it is that intellectuals, be they liberal or conservative, should never be overly esteemed. As Bill Buckley told us, we would be better governed by the first ten people you might meet on the sidewalk than by the entire faculty at Harvard University!

This lack of reasoned thought among the most educated members of our country is most clearly evidenced by the willingness in academic circles to rewrite history to accommodate current fads on diversity, Keynesian economics, and extreme environmental fears. Indeed, many of today's intellectual leaders appear to have reversed their definition—they act based on emotions, hope, peer pressure, feelings, and where the next grant is coming from—not on pure reason—the exact opposite of how intelligent life is supposed to function. For those students in Western colleges and universities, who must cope on a daily basis with the obvious inadequacies of today's favored textbooks and curricula, it can only be hoped that they will recall Captain Kirk's famous request, "Beam me up, Scotty. There's no intelligent life here."

The 2015 National Assessment of Educational Progress report shows that among our high school students, only 38 percent of twelfth-graders were proficient in reading, 26 percent in math, twelve percent in history, 20 percent in geography, and 24 percent in civics.[51] These results indicate that the school systems are failing to teach the basics needed to function in today's world. And our schools are run by the supposedly best and brightest! Perhaps our electricians and carpenters could do better?

Another report shows the pyramiding effect of this failure: among those high school graduates going on to college, The National Center for Public Policy and Higher Education reports that nearly 60 percent of first-year college students are not prepared for college-level studies. That means that in addition to the trillions spent on free or reduced tuition and student loans, colleges are obliged to spend billions of dollars on remedial education. This sad story is compounded by the fact that many of the students never graduate from college, even though many of the college courses have been dumbed down to make it easier to graduate!

Understand that a child's most formative years, when his or her skills and thinking ability are growing and are most receptive to learning, are spent in these deficient schools. The inadequacy of our schooling plays a major role in creating the inequality of our graduates in four ways:

First, by emphasizing grades and ignoring all the other qualities that will determine the child's success they are favoring those kids with abstract thinking and good memorization skills, while neglecting the potential talents of individuals with sound aptitudes to be artists, engineers, businessmen and mechanics. Indeed, any child that is average or worse in the ability to score well on grades is short changed.

Second, those children good at tests, regardless of their other qualities, are given a head start into the leadership roles that will most impact our nation's future. Yet many of them lack the over-all balance and judgment needed to provide good performance in those leadership roles.

Thirdly, by failing to drill home the basic fundamentals of reading, writing, and arithmetic, they leave many students without essential competencies.

> "The same man cannot well be skilled in everything; each has his own excellence."
>
> -Euripides, Rhesus
>
> (c. 455-441 B.C.)

Fourthly, by losing a large part of the age group altogether who just drop out and never finish school, they are adding to a permanent class divide that is a main source of our income inequality. We know people are not equal, but good schooling could reduce that inequality and especially help those at the bottom.

John Kao, a Harvard Business School professor, has sounded the alarm about America's decline. He explains in *Innovation Nation* how we are losing our competitive edge and that other technology savvy nations are passing us in innovation and discovery: "We are rapidly becoming the fat, complacent Detroit of nations...We are losing our collective sense of purpose along with our fire, ambition, and determination to achieve."[52] Truer words have rarely been written, but Kao's suggested remedies reflect the usual faulty thinking of an intellectual: he recommends government do something to stimulate innovation and improve our schools. He skips over the fact that we have been spending more and more on schools for over forty years with nothing to show for it. He avoids the hot button issue of how the government works with the teachers' unions to oppose alternative schools and efforts to improve teacher qualifications. And, he doesn't mention the need to help the many youngsters who do not even attend schools.

Experts like Kao can identify some of the problems in our schools (which are actually pretty obvious to everyone) but they have trouble escaping from the structured thinking which blinds them to effective solutions. The problems are too deep rooted to be fixed with band aids. It will require several bold moves that most professionals are afraid to even contemplate:

1.) Remove the unions' stranglehold on school regulations and policy.
2.) Eliminate the teachers' colleges' monopoly on the credentialing of teachers that restricts the quality and supply of teachers.

3.) Restore the teaching of useful educational subjects and eliminate ideological, religious, and political topics.

4.) Strip the federal and state departments of education of all but the most essential functions and leave teaching to local and state authorities.

5.) Remove obstacles that prevent new schools from attracting all types of students and let them cater to the different needs of children.

It is noteworthy that these kinds of "bold" moves call for no action other than the removal of current obstacles to good education! President Reagan was right about how government actions are not the solution, they are the problem! Of course, the "government" can't act—it's the experts in government that design these failed educational policies. The reforms needed to fix America will come, not from the government doing more, but from a new president merely stopping the ill-advised things the experts have had the government do. And that kind of cure costs nothing! Just close the Department of Education.

Kao is right in his observation that we have lost our "sense of purpose along with our fire, ambition, and determination to achieve." But he confuses the symptoms of our affliction with its causes, and therefore he seeks to cure the symptoms without addressing the underlying causes. The cure lies in restoring a sense of unity and purpose, igniting and rewarding fire and determination in our people. Instead our government rewards idleness, regulates and taxes initiative, welcomes divisive immigrants, and stirs up class divisions.

When America's people escaped the tyranny of former lands, and found freedom in the New World, they reveled in the opportunities afforded them. They had gained liberty, left the aristocracies and intellectuals behind, and were free to apply their genius and persistence to innovations and building a better future. And they did that for a couple hundred years. Indeed, the man often called America's first intellectual, Ralph Waldo Emerson, didn't appear for 250 years after our first settlers had arrived and built a great nation. Eventually, as generations succeeded generations, the experts arrived, our culture was attacked, a political correctness suppressed free speech, and the unique strength of the common people dissipated.

The weakening of the people's character has been accelerated by the academics and demagogues who denigrate American traditions, patriotism, and family values. Ben Stein has exposed the truth: "There's a sustained assault against America, *by* Americans...men and women paid for by inheritances, foundation grants, the astronomical salaries of Hollywood, and the U. S. Congress."[53] There is a new elite in the land, devoid of old values, intent on self-aggrandizement, and their theories are going to shackle our minds and make us follow the dictates of their growing bureaucracy. Can you blame a few of our presidential candidates for being outspoken and as angry as hell?

Chapter 16

SOCIALISM AND SAFETY NETS;
CAN COMPASSION LEAD TO TYRANNY?

I must preface this chapter by admitting that I do not know much about poverty although I did grow up during the Great Depression, and did experience the occasional pangs of hunger, financial insecurity, and the scorn of some snobby individuals in the community who considered themselves superior. Offsetting that position at the bottom, our poverty was fortunately defined only by our financial condition, for when it came to pride and self-respect we were the equal of anyone in town. Our optimism and dreams were reflected by my mother's advice "to hitch your wagon to a star," which seemed to me as a ten year old to be a perfectly logical and achievable goal.

A worse kind of poverty than I experienced is the poverty of the soul and I have seen that first-hand in other people who were in fact no worse off financially than my family. Such poverty is mostly in the mind and is much worse than just being broke, because the being broke kind can be fixed by work and persistence. Many biologists believe that the optimism and ambition needed to make one's way are built into each of us by our genes and our environment. It seems to me that there are a lot of kids in America who are getting a low dose of those valuable traits and that deficiency is causing some of the mental kind of poverty that is so hard to escape.

We have seen in earlier chapters that there is a growing problem with persistent poverty and that even thousands of government programs have failed to make things better. It is very possible that the mere existence of all those programs is expanding the need for more! Financial poverty can be cured—you just have to pay attention in school and find a job and that is certainly possible for many of the millions of people on the assistance rolls. But mental poverty can never be overcome without a different attitude, and the widely available and generous "entitlement" programs discourage the work needed to develop a sound attitude. Note that the euphemism "entitlement" represents a new view-that "welfare assistance" is owed to the recipient and has become a positive right to income. Dr. Dalrymple has noted the same trend among his poorest patients in England who will make comments about how they are "getting their paycheck" this week.

The culture was different in my youth. When the Selectmen stopped by, at the depth of the Great Depression, to ask my mother if she needed help she declined taking any. Years later, when my step-father became sixty-five, he was very reluctant to apply for his social security. It was customary to respect the old aphorisms that taught the value of hard work and persistence. Ben Franklin's sayings about thrift and the work ethic are no longer a part of our heritage. The educational establishment ignores them along with the Horatio Alger books that told of young boys going off to seek their fortune and then returning home to aid their parents. Those were cultural underpinning that have been shuffled aside, allowing cynicism to stifle the ambition of too many children. The advocates of big government do not want to encourage the idea of upward mobility—it would decrease their welfare work load.

Today, every American understands that there is a need for a safety-net to help those people truly in need. The differences that divide people on this subject are simply a matter of who should get help and how much should they get? But the public has become so polarized that many people see it differently: you are either for welfare or against it. This confused mess should not be a problem of ideology, it is not about whether we should or should not help the needy, it simply cries out for rational simplification and good management. Why can't we have just one, or even a couple, programs to help those in need?

Just ask yourself—do we really need hundreds of programs to administer America's safety net? In fact, there are over 2,000 "relief" programs and they have spiraled out of control. They are separately managed by hundreds of different federal and state agencies. Over one-third of the population now receives some form of assistance!

The food stamp program is one of the largest of the eighty (80!) means-tested welfare programs. The number of people receiving food stamps has risen from seventeen million in 2000 to forty-seven million in 2015. Within that group, the most rapid growth in food stamp recipients was among able bodied and work-capable adults between the ages of 18 and 49 with no dependents. That group of recipients has more than doubled under the Obama administration since 2008, increasing from 2 million to 5 million people.[54]

A few states have imposed a work requirement for those able-bodied recipients without dependents. In those states,

when asked to perform even the most minimal requirements for aid, most recipients chose to leave the program.
In Maine, most childless adult recipients refused to participate in job training programs or to perform just six hours
of community service per week. As a result, three months
after Maine's work requirement policy went into effect, its
caseload of food stamp recipients dropped by 80 percent![55]
Apparently, they weren't that needy.

It is not surprising that most federal operations are
poorly designed and poorly managed. Even the U. S. Army
famously gave us the term SNAFU, suggesting that the *normal* situation in government is a form of chaos. For example, the Social Security Administration's inspector general
recently reported that that agency does not have the technical ability to record death information on its computer.
That means they cannot correct their files for all the social
security "numberholders" who exceed "maximum reasonable life expectancies," including many people who were
born before the Civil War.

Their computer rolls, called in Washingtonian lingo,
their Numident data, recently identified approximately 6.5
million numberholders born before June 16, 1901 who did
not have a date of death on their record, and are therefore receiving social security benefit checks every month.
The inspector general also reported that the original social
security numbers that had been given to long-dead people

are being used fraudulently to open bank accounts and that thousands of those numbers were also used by illegal immigrants to obtain benefits and report wages.[56]

The increasing expansion and inefficiency of hundreds of assistance programs has continued under both Republican and Democratic administrations and the problem is rarely mentioned in campaign speeches. What is mentioned is the need for more and bigger programs. Yet, a recent study by the Cato Institute determined that in many states, welfare provides a bigger after-tax income than many jobs. If you look at just a few welfare programs you may get the false impression that welfare benefits are low. But, the federal government funds over a hundred separate programs for low-income people, and each State has additional programs. Cato's report concludes: "There are so many categories of welfare recipients and so many different types of benefits, that it is extremely difficult to determine how many people get what combination of benefits. "[57]

In thirty-nine states, a typical combination of federal and state benefits provides the recipient more than the starting wage for a secretary. In ten states, welfare pays more than the average pretax first-year wage for a teacher, and in the three most generous states, welfare benefits exceed the entry-level salary for a computer programmer.[58] And it's tax free!

Based on that data, one can understand why the Department of Health and Human Services reports that less than 42 percent of adult welfare recipients participate in work activities. "Poor people aren't stupid. If they can get more from the government than they can from a job, they aren't going to work."[59]

It has been suggested that most politicians want to extend the helping hand of government to more and more people, to get them dependent, and thereby advance the political power and financial well-being of the elites that run the government. If you watched the debates between Hillary Clinton and Bernie Sanders you can understand their battle is simply over which one will promise the most to their constituents-whether they need it or not.

Management Run Amuck!

Catalog of Federal Domestic Assistance (CFDA) contains detailed program descriptions for 2,315 Federal assistance programs. The following chart shows the program distribution for the top five issuing agencies.

523 Department of Health and Human Services-40%
278 Department of the Interior-21%
268 Department of Agriculture-20%
137 Department of Justice-10%
115 Department of Housing and Urban Development-9%

2,315   total programs

The more programs created to help people the more government workers are needed. All the employees and beneficiaries of these programs will be forever brought into the tent of the new nanny-loving segment of our people. A government by its very nature will grow whether it needs to or not because everyone working in government wants to not only keep his or her job, but expand their job and the size of his or her little fiefdom.

The fact that this expensive and inefficient part of our government has continued to spiral out of hand raises the question of whether voters are rational. Many people will enthusiastically support the campaigning politician who promises to "put a chicken in every pot." Many will support such a candidate regardless of the cost, or whether it can be done fairly or efficiently, or if even there is a need to do so. Bryan Caplan, for one, has argued that voters are not rational. He hedges that a little by saying that since each voter believes his or her one vote won't matter, they need not be rational. And, if the vote won't matter, the net result is that such voters will vote for what makes them feel good.[60] Whether it really is good simply doesn't matter. It's more a matter of simply feeling good about oneself.

Scott Adams, of Dilbert fame, has written persuasively that "If you believe people use reason for the important decisions in life, you will go through life feeling confused and frustrated that others seem to have no reasoning skills."[61] He argues that most people want to believe in things that make them feel good about themselves, even if they know those things to be false. That is why, even when they know a politician is lying, they may support him or her, and they will keep doing so even if they know that what is promised can never work! This mental anomaly was made especially clear by a devoted communist who admitted in the late 1980's an almost visceral *need to believe*. Gerda Lerna's story appeared earlier in chapter twelve and illustrates how far this need to believe can go in people of high intellect: Even after accepting communism's complete failure, she acknowledged, "I still had to believe in the dream." It was such a beautiful dream she could not live without it. But, as John Podhoretz confided, any ordinary common man or woman would know better immediately.

Myron Caplan also suggests that voters have biases that lead them to vote against many good policies: such voters may just be against free markets, have a disdain for patriotism, want totally free access to guns, or are emotionally opposed to the corporate sector. Voters holding such irrational biases will not vote at random, Caplan asserts, but will en masse decide who wins elections. A smaller, informed, rational minority will often lose the elections. Led by such biases and the desire to feel good, voters may get what they want, but what they want can often be bad for them, and the country, but many don't care!

Now, Caplan's and Scott's arguments can be faulted, but they do make sense. There are many ideological biases being formed by the school systems where academics, who are about 90 percent of the far left persuasion, shape the minds of students into being pro government and pro welfare in general. Unfortunately, that shaping of minds does not extend to teaching logic or a well reasoned analysis of political and social issues. The horrors of nuclear warfare and the bombing of Japan sixty years ago are taught without any discussion of the pros and cons of that decision. And nothing is taught concerning the positive contribution of corporate America, the source of new life-saving medicines, the availability of food, or how small businesses provide all the jobs in America outside the offices of government.

In short, people may vote irrationally because of biases, ignorance, conditioning, to feel good, or just due to disinterest. Nevertheless, they usually do bring more good sense to the conduct of their own lives. That is why, if the government programs make it more profitable to take aid than work, it is quite rational for many to do so. Taking food stamps, even finagling to get enrolled in a number of welfare programs, shows sound judgment for people with few job skills. If they have limited training, ambition, or ability, isn't it a mark of wisdom to take advantage of an overly generous welfare system?

Granted, it may make sense to take aid, but it also has made "cheats" out of a lot of Americans—it's called trickle-down immorality. In recent years, as unemployment figures declined, disability rolls soared. A 2013 article in the Baltimore Sun reported that: "Since President Obama's 2009 inauguration, 5.9 million people have been added to SSDI, a 23 percent increase over the last five years (compare that to 2.5 million new jobs created during the same time period); and SSDI rolls have swollen to almost 11 million recipients (translation: 1 in 14 U.S. workers). Thus, in a period when only 2.5 million new jobs were created, over twice as many people left the job market for disability coverage! The article reports that surveillance of applications was lax to accommodate new claims and of course it made unemployment figures look better by 5.9 million people. For all those new claimants, what they did may make sense—they are not irrational; they are just conning the elites at the top, and incidentally, killing America!

Peter Salins's book, *The Smart Society*, draws attention to the harm done by America's current assistance programs. He points out that these programs basically pay people not to work and motivate people to rely on public stipends instead.[62] As an accomplished educator, he recognizes the fact that anything that reduces our human capital and the motivation of people to contribute to the country will jeopardize our future. Salins defines human capital as the sum of the acquired personal abilities that help each person to be economically and socially useful.[63] Obviously, encouraging people not to work reduces the nation's capital.

Salins correctly defines "smart" as "not just in having a high IQ, but in any number of other functional or social ways."[64] And he correctly points out that America's success has always been built by the efforts of this large number of smart and productive citizens. Edith Piaf could have added to her caustic comment that the "smart" Frenchmen, who all went to America, also applied for disability benefits on arrival!

Salins points out that, while our public assistance programs show great compassion, the escalating numbers being assisted poses a warning: "The total cost of these programs is directly proportional to the percentage of the population with severely deficient human capital."[65] The truth is that today about half the people rely on the government for much of their income, and the entitlement costs are breaking the nation's bank. The other truth is that most of these people are not "severely deficient" but are in effect made so by overly generous welfare assistance that pays them not to work.

The pressures and stress from modern lifestyles, the anonymity of urban living, and the masses of people crowded into smaller spaces, have impaired the original support systems and added to the number who feel powerless and without any control over their lives. These changes in our society are a portent of things to come. Knowing the inefficiency and inadequacy of government programs, what will these assistance programs look like in fifty years or another hundred years when there are over a hundred million more people to care for? That will no longer be America as we know her!

Professor Seligman's 1975 book, *Helplessness,* showed the damage done by "learned helplessness," the growing belief by many that they are helpless. Such an attitude leads to a feeling that responding on your own to challenges is useless, and that leads to feelings of despair, lethargy, and dependency. It has been subsequently shown that such feelings impact not only our behavior, but our health.

Now, while we know that there are individual differences in one's ability to act and take control of situations, any culturally endorsed belief that one cannot act sufficiently on his or her own, but needs help, will create more victims. And we have all seen the people in store check-out lines using their food stamps and EBT cards who appear vigorous and healthy and perfectly able to work and earn a living. Many seem to have come to believe that such aid is their right—it's actually an "entitlement!"

> "I am for doing good to the poor,
>
> but I differ in opinion of the means.
>
> I think the best way of doing good
>
> is not making them easy in poverty,
>
> but leading or driving them out of it.
>
> -Benjamin Franklin

Peter Salins suggests that the way to turn these problems around is to provide more education, especially intensive pre-school for three and four year olds, five days a week. He refers to the large numbers of lower to middle class children who fail to benefit from our public schools as a megagap, and it is caused by "familial socio-economic circumstances."[66] The problem he writes is that the families in which they are raised, poor and headed predominantly by single mothers,fail to give their children the kinds of cognitive and emotional stimulation necessary for early childhood development that their more fortunate upper-middle-class peers on the far side of the megagap are able to get at home. This is not a small problem—in 2011 there were about 74 million children under 17 years of age in America and about one-third lived in single parent households.

Salins reminds his readers that attempts to improve schools—racial integration, spending more, higher teacher salaries, and reducing class size—have all failed to improve results. It is the cultural illiteracy caused by growing up in dysfunctional homes that prevents such children from competing with those from traditional and more affluent families. It is that divide that keeps increasing income inequality.

Professor Salins recommendations are twofold: (1)To provide pre-school to all children that will provide a wholesome learning environment that they do not get at home, and, (2) to promote policies that will *motivate* students to study and learn. Professor Salins, even as a conservative, is asking for the government to solve this problem by basically replacing the time kids spend with their dysfunctional families with more time in government school programs. He also wants the government to find a way to motivate people that lack motivation. Such proposed "cures" for America's malaise show the problem we face. Many actually believe the government can cure the problems it created!

Neither of these needs for pre-school and "creating" motivation were present in America from 1620 to 1920, during the three hundred year period before the progressive movement started down the road of taking care of people's every need. We have been blindsided by two destructive forces: a growing government taking over the family's responsibility and the related huge dystopic growth in the population of people and dysfunctional families. Aside from the harmful impact of the government, we have seen both a cultural and genetic deterioration. Our original work-oriented and religious culture has been weakened by those who preach multi-culturalism, dependency, and moral relativity.

Michael Gazzaniga writes that the original cultural standard of independence and self-reliance is passing, with more and more Americans demonstrating a passive attitude, and learned helplessness. Aside from the harmful effect this has on the workforce, such weakness has been linked to a host of diseases including cancer, heart disease, arthritis, and diminished immune function. Apparently, the extent to which you feel in control not only affects your attitude but also impacts your physical health.

Gazzaniga writes: "Clearly, the brain mechanism that allows for the feeling of control is one that has considerable survival power and thus must have been selected for in evolution. With this in mind, society must examine the social programs, policies, and institutions that, although established to provide and care for us, actually minimize our influence over our environment: That is, such programs as welfare and institutions for the elderly, may actually, in disempowering the individual, be detrimental to one's mental and physical well-being."[67]

In today's Politically Correct culture, Gazzaniga's warnings are at risk of being dismissed as mean-spirited. Public dialogue is frozen into a child-like stubbornness, an irrational inability to approach things rationally, and make considered judgments. And yet the public assistance problem will only get worse unless something is done. That is why, in order to force a reasonable solution, populist democracies have sometimes taken refuge under strong minded leaders who are prepared to cut to the chase and make hard decisions.

Sometimes simple, arbitrary, and resolute decisiveness is needed. Could an experienced manager like Chris Christie, John Kasich, or Donald Trump be the type of person to do this? As full time managers they have skipped a lot of the rhetoric and accomplished real-world tasks. The senators have just talked, and talked, and talked! Sooner or later, a competent administrator will be needed, and mightn't that be the only type of solution to solve today's intractable problems? Otherwise, you may have to wait until Nancy Pelosi and Marco Rubio, Ted Cruz, or Jeb Bush achieve a polite meeting of the minds and clean up this mess? Could you live that long?

Chapter 17

DEMOGRAPHICS;
THE PROBLEM WITH PEOPLE

Thomas Robert Malthus described a frightening future for mankind back in 1798 when he predicted the inevitability of famines and disease from over-population. Ever since he threw that bombshell, his disciples have sought to find every way to encourage birth control, abortions, and governmental action to avoid an overpopulation catastrophe. As a result of these fears there has been success in slowing the spiraling population increase, but only in some nations. As a result the efforts to limit growth are creating major shifts in population between regions and within nations. What's happening is that the more successful and affluent people are having less children and the less successful and less affluent are having more.

Current trends show that Africans will represent a much larger percent of the world's future population and whites a smaller percentage due to the altered fertility rates. And within America, some writers have pointed out that our welfare assistance programs are rewarding large families in the bottom socio-economic levels with subsidies, while those families most able to rear their children are reducing the size of their families. Another way of looking at this is that an ever larger proportion of American children are being raised in households that are the least able to nurture them to responsible adulthood. That trend will likely result in an ever-larger and larger dependent class needing to be supported.

> "I think that God, in creating man, somewhat overestimated his ability."
>
> Oscar Wilde

When Malthus started all these fears, he was influenced by the huge increases in England's population during the preceding fifty years of the eighteenth century. He argued that population was increasing faster than food production. However, his theories have proven wrong. So far, the twentieth century advances in agricultural practices have greatly increased food supply and kept up with population increases.

To the extent that there is a problem, it hasn't been one of supply so much as an inequality of distribution. We have seen some nations destroying crops or giving away surpluses, while the people of other nations starve. Famines have been fearsome in many nations but they have been caused by political disturbances—mostly by the lack of safety—and not by an inability to produce food. The people of many nations in need are not even able to protect or distribute what's given to them due to rampant lawlessness and civil strife.

Malthus's main failing was not in his assertion that growing populations are a problem, but in his reasoning why it is a problem. Julian Simon, P. T. Bauer, and others have shown that human ingenuity and the marvels of their innovations can provide for almost anything we need. They point out that it is the people in a nation that are its ultimate resource,[68] not its climate, minerals, rivers, or arable land. What Malthus missed was not the problem of feeding expanded populations, but the problem of organizing them, policing them, and providing wholesome environments for them.[69]

One of many lessons of history seems to be that as democracies get larger, their expanded numbers get divided into sparring groups, become confused by the ideologies and theories of "experts," lose their cultural identity, and get bankrupted by debts. Such nations may have plenty to eat, but nevertheless, when their population gets too big, they seem to stagnate or decline.

That decline of large successful nations has usually been accelerated by the twin sins of excess internal corruption and over-extension into exhausting foreign entanglements. All of these negative developments are evident in America today. It is very possible that a democracy can be too big. The question is whether we have reached a size and a condition where our nation is ungovernable and cannot function well any longer in the current democratic form?

The founding fathers, when they were first creating the newly free American government, were not too concerned over its size or its future growth. They did know that what they were fashioning had to rule over the vast areas of the thirteen colonies and probably much of the North American continent in the future. History had seen many republics they could look to and emulate, but none were as large as the one they were dealing with. However, their initial intention was displayed in the Articles of Confederation, written in 1777, which provided for a very decentralized system of government built around the sanctity of states' rights. The Founders knew that a powerful central government could be as big a threat to their freedom as the English King had been.

However, within ten years of adopting the Articles of Confederation, many of the American leaders became dissatisfied with the loose ties in that arrangement and called a convention to write a new federal constitution. The objective was to establish a stronger republic, which would grant more power to the central powers in the Capital and that's what they did. Now, after more than two hundred years have gone by, the central government is taking more and more power unto itself and a politicized Supreme Court does little to resist this consolidation of power in Washington.

Population growth may not have us going hungry, but it has stirred controversy concerning immigration. Proposals to restrict fertility rates have recently been turned on their head by concern over the plight of refugees and illegal immigrants. Ironically, policies allowing large numbers of new entrants co-exist with policies seeking fewer children and subsidizing Planned Parenthood's virtually unrestricted abortions. The net result is that we are seeing a rapid growth in our population, not from the American babies that might have been allowed to live, but from unknown and unskilled foreign immigrants and Muslim refugees. For those who like "diversity," that may be a desirable outcome, but the eventual effect on the nature of our people and their culture will probably be negative. And the bottom line is that these contrary and confused policies are still allowing the population to spiral upward.

The topic of immigration and population size reveals the confusion of our government, overwhelmed by the sheer numbers of people involved and their inconsistency of policy. The State Department makes it very difficult for self-supporting professionals to enter the country, but, in an excess of "tolerance," permits low-skill illegal immigrants and welcomes Muslim refugees. They put up obstacles for those with sound credentials while allowing many with poor credentials an easy entry to America! Just the opposite of what rational people should do!

The resulting growth in population and the diversity of the people has surpassed anything the Founders might have expected. Tolerating cultural and religious diversity, in excess, can undermine a successful culture. There is a serious question today whether adherents of Islam, with their culture that condones the suppression of women, their refusal to separate religion from government, and their demand for Sharia law, can ever become part of the American dream that opposes all those beliefs. If not, their influence will add to internal turmoil and create confusion over just what it means to be an American. When that cultural conflict emerges, America will no longer be America as we have known her. As Robert H. Frank writes, "tolerance, like any of the other virtues, is not absolute." [70]

Ironically, twenty to thirty years ago, excess population was the subject of a major political controversy, with most people concerned about the danger from unrestrained growth. Today, the pendulum has swung and the controversy centers on allowing millions of immigrants to add to our population problems. These opposing issues are at the heart of the five divisive forces creating the current destructive ideological battles in America:

First, the sheer size of the government reduces transparency and increases the opportunity for secret deals and unfair subsidies to segments of the voting public. Financial and budgetary management gets lost in the shuffle and deficits balloon the national debt.

Second, the diversity of race, religion, and customs creates a citizenry with widely different objectives that destroys traditional ideas of team work and cooperation.

Third, an ever-larger and more diverse population shatters the traditional culture, creating serious rifts among groups of people, each competing for its own interests.

Four, the elected leaders are so torn between all the competing interests, and the need to pacify all, that they become locked in a partisan struggle that precludes decisive action. Ideological battles trump sound management of the government.

Five, the political chaos that develops, and the complexity of the huge bureaucracy, provide a perfect cover for corruption. It is arguable that corruption has grown faster than the population, a possibility that may have Malthus turning over in his grave, wishing he had equated graft instead of hunger as the result of unmitigated population expansion.

These problems will not go away easily. The question remains unanswered on whether we will be able to maintain equality and liberty under a massive central bureaucracy with four hundred million people, but it seems doubtful unless changes are made. If there was a way to hope for a continued viable democratic system it would have to first, minimize the divisive ideological battles over social issues, maybe turn them over to each state to handle; second, curb the corruption and campaign financing abuses; and, third, reduce the overwhelming one size fits all mandates of the central government.

If more power were transferred to each state, the political system would become more transparent and more subject to voter review. Campaigns would become less costly, and innovative efficiencies developed by the fifty independent states would be possible, and winning solutions could be copied by others. Most importantly, we could eliminate federal subsidies and most of the federal agencies that impose their control and expense on all the states and individuals of the country.

In short, there's plenty of food to go around, but as far as numbers go, and people, we just have too many of them.

And what's worse, there is no evidence that the people are getting smarter, more honest, harder working, more self-reliant, or more attentive to good government. Take note that our Greatest Generation dates back to more than sixty years ago! Those are among the reasons why a nation should be very careful about who gets let in and who is kept out. Sensible immigration laws have been enforced by all countries for a long time-and when you already have too many people, it makes a lot of sense to enforce some limits on both the numbers and the quality of those admitted. But can you even imagine what kind of a president it would take to actually do something about all that?

Chapter 18

IS THERE AN ACCEPTABLE DEGREE OF INCOME INEQUALITY?

Peter Salins's book, *The Smart Society*, describes the government programs of the last fifty years that were designed to alleviate income inequality, and concludes that they have all failed to make any significant improvement.[71] This continued failure is probably apparent to most voters, so why do they keep electing the same kinds of politicians who have such a poor record? It seems that the worse things get, the more willing voters are to believe the politicians' promises to make things better. It makes one wonder whether the voting public is made up of rational beings. They keep electing leaders who have created and maintained this unfair, corrupt, almost bankrupt situation that we find ourselves in today.

Since 1944 the people in the bottom 90 percent have seen their share of national income shrink from 67 percent of total income to only 49 percent. And the share taken by the top 1% has kept increasing, even during President Obama's term in office. Today's elected leaders show no indication that they intend to even try and reverse this trend that is increasing the large inequality in incomes.

The voters apparently don't see that our problems are largely the result of the politicians' prior efforts to make things better! Take poverty: the War on Poverty, dating back to President Johnson in the 1960s, has failed to alleviate poverty but, by subsidizing the children living in poverty, has created more of them. Our meddling in foreign policy has disrupted most of the countries in the Middle East so that they are all in turmoil, with millions of people killed, and no improvement in sight. Forced integration in the big cities prompted a White flight to the suburbs that resulted in inner cities less integrated than before. Deregulation in the financial industry relaxed the rules against speculative trading and sub-prime mortgages, gave tax breaks to the speculators, all while burying the smaller banks with the requirements of more paperwork. Maintaining almost zero interest rates on savings to help the economy recover from the mortgage melt-down only served to enrich the bankers while cheating the thrifty of income on their savings. It is not a winning record to be proud of.

Joseph Stiglitz's recent book, *The Great Divide*, reviews the growing problem of income inequality in America, and suggests a number of ways to reduce it. About half the "solutions" require the government to stop doing things that have expanded the degree of inequality. These are the unfair policies that have tilted the playing field against ordinary people in favor of the well connected. The other half of his suggestions call for the government to do more to help those at the bottom. The obvious conclusion from reading his book is that the government is doing too many bad things and not enough good things. That's not surprising! As President Ronald Reagan said, "Government is the problem!"

Stiglitz cites Brooking Institute research that shows: "only 58 percent of Americans born into the bottom fifth of income earners move out of that category, and just 6 percent born into the bottom fifth move into the top." Note that he uses the words "only" and "just" to imply there is no longer any upward mobility in America. Another way of looking at these numbers is that more than half those born into the bottom fifth do move up! And, since we're talking about individuals, that means that within each generation more than half move up. Is that glass half-full or half-empty?

Those statistics actually come as a pleasant surprise—that so much upward mobility still exists in America. Most pundits and politicians have been claiming that upward mobility is no longer possible in America. But it seems that any child born into the bottom fifth, has a better than even chance of moving up, and if he fails to do so, his children will still have that same possibility of moving up. On the face of it that sounds pretty good. And, don't despair that almost one-half remain in the bottom fifth. After all, if over half move up, another group, almost half a quintile, must move down to the bottom quintile! Statistically, there will always be a bottom 20 percent, even if they are all millionaires, and there is no way to get rid of that situation. It's just arithmetic. What concerns everybody is simply the degree of inequality and the fact that some of the top 1 percent are getting an unfair and undeserved slice of the pie.

In his chapter entitled "Causes of America's Growing Inequality," Stiglitz writes about how the tax system is stacked against the 99 percent and helps the rich get richer. He ignores the fact that almost half of Americans pay no taxes; and thus he avoids facing the truth that the tax system actually rewards both the top 1 percent and the bottom 50 percent! So, in fact we have the very unfair situation where 49 percent of the people are supporting the other 51 percent either by direct subsidies or the granting of tax loopholes. The unfairness of this situation is indicated by the fact that those at the bottom are still needy, but the 1 percent is grossly well off, piling up tens, even hundreds, of millions of dollars a year, much of it from financial manipulations that do not even contribute products or useful services to the economy.

An alarming trend is also occurring within the bottom 50 percent. The number of those people who receive aid is getting larger each year, as more and more people leave the workforce, and opt out, claiming disability, welfare, social security, or one of dozens of forms of government assistance. The inequity wasn't so bad fifty years ago, when there were about 70 percent of the people supporting the other 30 percent. But, during the last seven years under President Obama, the number receiving help increased dramatically and it appears destined to keep increasing as it has for years. Because middle class families are paying out almost half their income in taxes and fees, with both husband and wife working, and the cost of living increasing, some of them each year will be tempted or forced to join those who live, at least in part, off the government. But can you blame them for taking the easier path? It is the government policies that tempt them to do so.

We know that it is rational, in one's own affairs, to think long-term, but for the relatively unskilled and poorly schooled individuals, stuck in an impoverishing environment, it is simple common sense to take whatever benefits are offered. After all, if the system is unfair and corrupt, why not join the party? That is why some pundits warn that the growth in welfare dependency is related to the level of corruption in government. It might be termed "trickle down morality!"

Most people accept the fact that some individuals will have more than others. Thus, the inequality of income and wealth is not always a serious issue that divides people. Almost all of our earliest settlers came from lands ruled over by aristocracies with wide disparities in wealth. And much of that inequality was undeserved-due simply to one's birth into the ranks of the landed gentry. No wonder that there was a flood of emigrants leaving England in the 1600s to seek opportunity in the American colonies! Those pioneers built our culture on the bedrock of fairness and justice; earned success was respected, albeit sometimes begrudgingly. And their efforts propelled America's economy so well that almost everyone shared a constantly increasing prosperity. Those people thought long-term; they worked to leave their children a richer and better life. And the resulting extraordinary forward progression carried us forward with its success for over three hundred years, before the rot started to settle in.

It is worth noting that income inequality has gotten inexcusably large with a democratic government in charge—a government that is supposed to care for the common people! And that has occurred under presidents Clinton, Bush, and Obama, the presidents who have had full executive power for the last twenty-four years. Can anyone believe the latest promises to fix everything! Bernie Sanders's and Ms Clinton's debates are all about who will give more goodies to the voters. But, would that help or hurt? How would it clean out the corruption? How would it make the federal agencies more efficient? Both political party's leaders have been expanding aid programs for fifty years, during which time inequality has continually increased, and the top 10 percent even today keep getting a larger slice of the pie!

Considering that, isn't it clear that we need a drastic change; a president who knows how efficient and honest organizations work and is not afraid of stepping on toes to get there? When we find such a man you cannot complain that he is angry, outspoken, even at times outrageous, because that is what it will take to fix all that is wrong.

PART V

THE FUTURE - WHERE

ARE WE GOING ??

Chapter 19

THE NEED FOR PROPER MEASURES OF MAN

Every spring, the March Madness basketball program brings together about fifty of the top college basketball teams in the country to compete for the national championship. Almost everyone that follows the sport knows at the outset the names of the six or seven most likely winners. And the coaches all know the names of the best players. They have watched them in high school, interviewed them, invited them to training camps, watched videos of them on the court, and prepared every week to play with or against them in college competition. When these students graduate from college, to enter the professional leagues, they are clearly ranked as first pick, second pick, and so on. When it comes to their ability at a sport, our youth can be ranked very accurately. But in our schools, which are arguably more vital to the nation's future, there is no attempt to evaluate a student's future or even his or her over-all ability.

The problem in the schools is that the educators have no standard by which to measure students other than by their grades on tests and homework. And the tests merely measure students' ability to regurgitate some memorized facts or run some numbers for the math questions. That might make sense if success in their future lives was going to depend on their memory and arithmetic skill. But we all know those things have little to do with adult life, one's success, or one's happiness.

Tests are useful to determine a student's progress in learning the basic reading, writing, and arithmetic skills, especially in the first six grades where those skills are supposed to be taught. But they are really tests not of students' abilities but of whether the teachers have done their job of teaching. The same is true of tests in high school: they serve primarily as a measure of teacher performance. They also help college admission personnel know which students could benefit from the particular courses offered at their college. But the tests cannot indicate which students will do well in the real world, in business, design, teaching, politics, law, and so on. That is because the personal qualities needed for such success go significantly beyond the ones measured by school grades, SAT scores, and IQ numbers.

Dr. R. J. Williams has shown that there are many variables in a person's total capability and we not only have trouble identifying them, but have no clue how to measure them. Williams states that "to classify members of the human family as either intelligent or dumb may be convenient for some purposes, but it is not justified by the scientific facts. Much less is it justified to classify individuals in the upper ranges as smart, smarter, or smartest."[72]

However, high grades play a big part in determining a child's future. Those who get good grades are admitted into the best colleges, and on graduation they get the best jobs. This bias in our educational culture creates an unequal status for those children endowed with great abilities other than getting good grades. They are ignored while those favored simply owing to their grades, become more learned and successful than those left behind. And they end up earning more than anyone else! Could there be a self-fulfilling fallacy here? Could there be an injustice here?

The problem is that our educators are part of a professional establishment that fails to measure their students' real potential and in turn fails to teach all the skills that are needed for success. They simply reward the students who are best at memorization and quickest with numbers. Daniel Goleman[73] has criticized this process and believes educators are concentrating on the few students who possess the least valuable cognitive traits: the high IQ types who, outside the physical sciences, are of dubious value. By concentrating on grades, no one is nurturing the other 80 percent of our children's capabilities.

Robert Sternberg has suggested we go to a three-headed analysis of intelligence:

1.) Analytic intelligence is similar to existing IQ tests.
2.) Creative intelligence represents one's creativity and imagination of a practical and useful kind.
3.) Practical intelligence is the ability to apply solutions to practical problems in a real-world environment.[74]

Other writers have called for evaluation of the ability to make decisions under uncertainty. Howard Gardner lists eight forms of intelligence, two of which include self-control, personal awareness, empathy, and social skills.[75] In The Millionaire Mind, Dr Stanley reports that most of the self-made millionaires that he studied emphasized the importance of tenacity over IQ.[76] As Thomas Edison quipped, "Genius is 99 percent perspiration and 1 percent inspiration." Coach Wooden's Pyramid of Success" is made up of fifteen blocks, almost all of which measure such intangibles as resilience, persistence, long-range viewpoint, and team work. Yet our educational establishment only looks at grades! Perhaps that is because those experts in education got their "advisory" positions simply for having good grades themselves. If so, that would explain why they can't fix our schools!

As we saw in earlier chapters there have been hundreds of important human traits identified. Allport and Odbert, for example, have collected all the words in the English language that designate distinctive behavior. They catalogued 17,953 such words! About a quarter were specifically used to describe persistent traits.[77] And experts have attempted to create tests to measure over three hundred traits considered important in a person's behavior. Williams concludes that the idea that "any one single characteristic is so outstandingly important as to be enthroned above all others is not only scientifically erroneous but in some cases vicious."[78]

> "Intellectual morons are the cognitive Elite who champion idiotic ideas and theories. They are the 'smart' people that fall for stupid ideas. Ph.D.'s, high IQs, and intellectual honors are not antidotes to thick-headedness."
>
> ----Daniel J. Flynn

Keith E. Stanovich has looked at the rational decision-making skills that have a big effect on success. As we all know only too well, some of us are more or less prone to errors of judgment! He asserts that there are certain attributes of intelligence that determine a person's decision-making ability, and that none of them are measured on IQ and SAT tests.

The unfortunate concentration by educators on only a portion of a person's talents reflects their own mistaken belief of what is important in life. They like abstract thinking and the ability to quickly grasp conceptual possibilities. They were good at it, and that limited but impressive ability got them jobs in academia. But the elevation of abstract thinkers to the elites of the land increases inequality. Every child has the potential to be good at something. Just a few helpful characteristics may vault him or her into action at the right time—bhgif he or she is aware of his or her possibilities and employ the needed work, planning, and persistence for the task. Our schools do nothing to promote such awareness in their students.

The academics who design the tests have made substantial changes in the cognitive skills required to score well, but, predictably, they have made the wrong kind of changes. As President Obama's administration has demonstrated, *change* is not always helpful. For example, educators have for years consistently altered the SAT tests to reward abstract thinking at the expense of concrete thinking. Academics see this change as freeing logic from the limits of concrete reality to deal with hypothetical questions and symbols. But, such a change is proving to be unfortunate. Many of the theories that have emerged from the abstract minds of experts have done more harm than good. James R. Flynn reports how school children used to be tested on their knowledge of culturally valued information, but that today tests only expect superficial knowledge of such information and are tested instead on understanding complex relationships between abstract concepts.[79] This change reflects the bias of academics who, (1) don't want to affirm our culture that they consider evil, and (2) overestimate the value of their conceptual virtuosity and seek to promote philosophers rather than mechanics. This process, and the advancement of high IQ types, has changed our leadership from practical minded people to those with an abstract and utopian vision of how they can make things better.

The new emphasis on abstract thinking has created a de facto segregation of the population that is unfair to the many very valuable "average" students. After all, almost all new businesses are created and run by average students, whereas abstract thinkers are generally employed in non-productive advisory and research establishments that do not *make* anything.

Furthermore, it is not clear whether the added power gained by abstract thinkers has helped in governing the political and social affairs of nations. If we compare today's soft-science elite to those of ancient republics we can only conclude that progress has eluded twenty-five centuries of soft-science intellectuals! From what we can read about the people of ancient Greece, Rome, Renaissance Italy, and Shakespeare's England, we are not

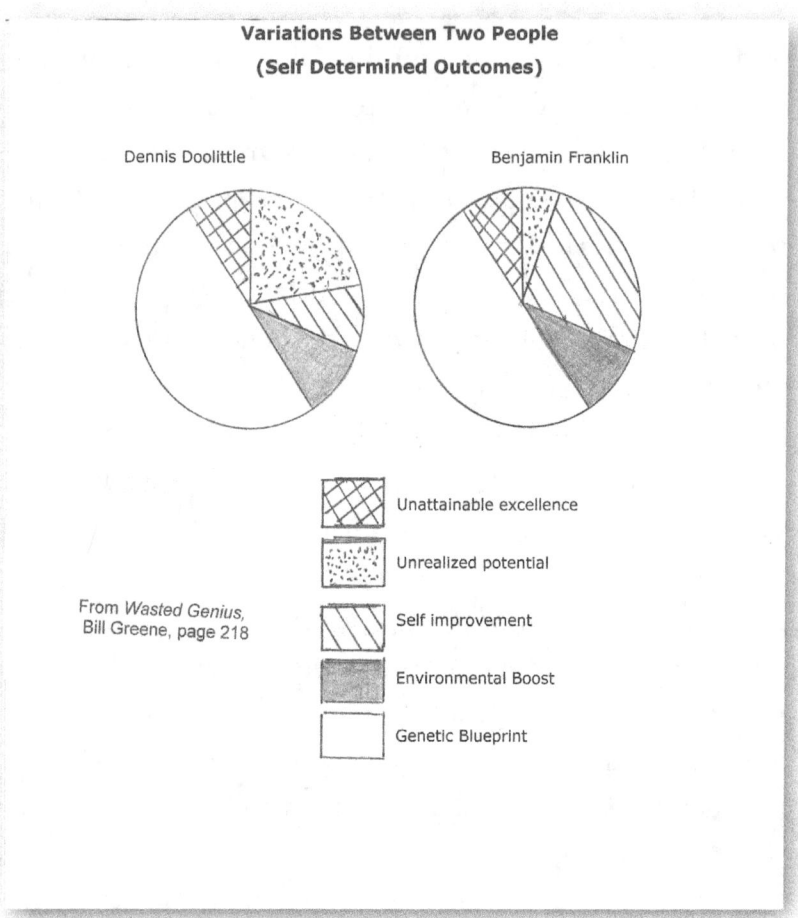

Variations Between Two People
(Self Determined Outcomes)

Dennis Doolittle　　　　　　Benjamin Franklin

Unattainable excellence

Unrealized potential

Self improvement

Environmental Boost

Genetic Blueprint

From *Wasted Genius,*
Bill Greene, page 218

The Five Parts of Total Potential Competency-TCQ

happier, shrewder, or more able to deal with life and matters of state than those ancient ancestors. The statesmen of Athens and Rome were every bit as wise and knowledgeable as ours are today. There is no evidence to show any advance in the art of governing. Indeed, recent events in Washington and Wall Street would indicate that we have too many abstract economic and political *theories* and corruption--and not enough common sense and integrity.

In most societies where the historical growth of technologies flourished, there were few intellectuals in residence. Only after the common people had built a prosperous society could intellectuals appear and be supported in their non-productive roles. Thus, it was the people with strong non-IQ parts of their brains that created most of the material advances we enjoy. Current trends to replace them with an abstract-minded leadership is both an injustice to others, and also a heavy burden to the society involved.

What is needed in the future if we are to come to understand the nature of man and his societies, is a measure of total competence. This could be labeled "TCQ" for total competency quotient. In *Wasted Genius,* it is suggested that TCQ is built from: 20 percent IQ, 20 percent EQ, 15 percent cultural beliefs, 15 percent motivational energy, and 30 percent personal attitudes and traits.[80] Aside from the cultural underpinnings, the other building blocks are mostly inherited, but each can be influenced, for better or worse, by the environment and self-disciplined effort.

Thus, if you think of a bar chart, with a TCQ at the top of a column, there would be, starting at the bottom, 50 percent from one's genetic blueprint, some additional competence from the environment, plus some more from self-improvement. The remaining unfilled area of the column would be made up of "unrealized potential." Someone like

Ben Franklin would have had a very small "unattained" area, and a large self-improvement gain. Others may have a large environmental boost, but little self-improvement. And some people gain little from either their environment or efforts at self-improvement! It is also possible that the environment could be a negative factor, and he or she will end up below their genetic foundation-literally below their starting point! In the illustration you can see that Dennis Doolittle made very little effort at self-improvement and must live with a lot of unrealized potential. Thus, each person's final level of accomplishment at maturity will vary greatly; and, that variation will depend largely on their family and themselves.

While the weight to be given each trait is unknown, the important traits to measure include self-restraint, emotional control, persistence, initiative, logical decision-making, resilience, intuition, patience, drive, and probably, a sense of humor. Such evaluations will tell what fields of work are most suitable for an individual and would help in creating more income equality rather than just letting many talents go wasted. The scales also indicate what positions a person will not be good at. Regardless of their high IQ and EQ, we should beware of those people with low common sense, poor decision-making skills, and/or a love of abstract ideologies, carefully separating them from authoritarian positions so that their arrogant impulses are not given the opportunity to usurp power over the rest of us.

These problems in the field of education are caused by the same ideological confusion that clouds all areas of our government. Most professional educators and their adherents are ideologically driven to instill certain partisan notions in the heads of their students. The vast majority of educators in our public schools and colleges are strong supporters of the Democratic Party, and have allowed political doctrines to take the place of necessary instruction in basic academic skills. Imposing such cultural orthodoxy into the minds of children is what has held back the people living under the rigid theocracy of Muslim nations. Similarly, it is holding back our students who need a better education than having social studies and history re-interpreted by ideologues who seek to pass on a partisan view of the world we all must live in.

Education must be free of ideology and its primary goal must be aimed at achieving some minimum level of knowledge, ethical values, and skills in *every* student. It should not give special attention to those with good memories, but instead should seek to include all children in the task and satisfaction of self improvement. By removing the ideology, and the preferred treatment of certain types of students we would be half way to decent schools.

Chapter 20

EUGENICS AND ALL THAT; POPULATION CONTROL

When it comes to reducing the surplus population, there has been remarkable success in America, but, unfortunately, the reduction has occurred primarily in those families most capable of properly nurturing their young. They have voluntarily reduced their family size. The bad news is that they are the only ones who have done this. As a result, those responsible and competent families have to work harder and pay more taxes to support the other part of the population which has kept producing more and more children.

The average American woman has 2.1 children which is about perfect to maintain the population with a very modest increase. But, because the American fertility rate is an average, it obscures the big class divide in fertility. The upper income classes have a negative fertility rate, while the lower economic classes have a positive reproduction rate. This represents a reversal of the way that the law of survival of the fittest functioned during the past 10,000 year.

In 2010, households with incomes in excess of $35,000 had birth rates of only fifty-five children per thousand women, while households with income under $10,000 had ninety-eight children per thousand women or almost twice as many.[81] The trend is that today, compared to past years, America's mothers are older, less likely to be married, and less likely to be either white or in the upper economic classes.

It should come as no surprise that the government's actions to discourage reproduction has created this dysgenic trend in America. The greatly expanded entitlement programs have allowed the fertility race to be won by those least able to care for or raise their offspring—they were paid to do just that! Meanwhile, well educated women increasingly entering the workforce have reduced their fertility rates to a less-than-replacement rate, while the rise in illegitimacy has increased the number of children disadvantaged by an inferior family environment.

These trends have worked to decrease the number of children from households which give their kids a head start and increase the numbers from those that give them a poor start. Result: the level of income inequality goes up, the proportion of children from dysfunctional homes goes up, and the average quality of America's human capital goes down.

There was a popular movement in the early twentieth century to direct human fertility in supposedly constructive ways. The popularity of such eugenic practices was fashionable among some intellectuals of the time because it offered a way to improve the human capital of a nation. However, such ideas went out of favor after the genocidal horrors of World War II and the bad example set by Hitler's ideas about a "master race." But milder efforts to control fertility, such as contraception and abortions, continued to gain favor to this day. The Supreme Court has upheld the right to birth control and abortion practices that are essentially the first step in eugenics. And developments in "assisted suicides" and euthanasia are still being advanced as reasonable medical practice. While euthanasia appears abhorrent to most people, it has been, and still is supported by many.

There is a professor at Princeton who is suggesting to his students that not only is abortion morally justified right up to the date of delivery, but that it may be perfectly acceptable to euthanize even one and two year old infants if it is clear that their future lives would be painful or costly due to their physical or mental health problems. Ironically, professor Singer is that university's *professor of biological ethics* and he has even argued that a healthy young pig's life is more to be valued than that of an impaired human infant. His theories are a good illustration of the damage done by abstract thinking, divorced from the constraints of Christian morality, and further reason to believe that many academics do more harm than good! But it is also a look ahead at where our elites are headed and the bleak future that threatens our children's lives.

The assisted suicide movement was recently led by Jack Kevorkian, but there are many advocates behind the scene financing and publicizing that form of euthanasia. An excellent survey of the movement and its prominent backers has been developed by Dr. Richard Fenigsen who practiced cardiology in the Netherlands where he witnessed the results of legalized euthanasia and documents in his book how fully competent patients were put to death without their permission by administering an overdose of drugs. He has outlined the future as a transformed world where euthanasia is accepted as part of an emerging Killing Society. In particular he describes the work of Peter Singer,[82] the current professor of bioethics at Princeton University who has written extensively in support of euthanasia.

Dr. Fenigsen points out that such practices will become a choice only for a society and a world quite different from the one we know—it will change the role and thinking of all doctors and that "the legalization of euthanasia will ultimately require a change in the system of government now prevailing in Western nations."[83] If you dislike the idea of capital punishment for heinous criminals, how will you take to killing grandma just because she becomes burdensome? But such decisions over life and death will inevitably result from the further centralization of power in a huge bureaucratic government that "administers" health care. Remember that we are on course to add one hundred million people to the American population in the next few decades, and old people will become a significant cost to be borne by the ever-fewer people still working. As Sarah Palin rashly quipped, "Grandma will die!" Ms Palin is a controversial figure, and she has been marginalized by the liberal media, but she does say it like it is, uncomfortable as that may be!

A much more reasonable form of eugenics was advocated by Margaret Sanger in 1921 when she founded the American Birth Control League to advocate birth control practices. In 1942 the name was changed to Planned Parenthood Federation of America. At the time, most of the leaders of the group were already involved in the eugenics movement, a group founded on the belief that certain classes of people were "unfit" and should be eliminated. The stated purpose of the organization was simply to advise women on their reproductive choices, but Sanger's activities almost one hundred years ago drew criticism. She created a program called the "Negro Project," which appeared to some as racially driven. Her ideas took firm root and the organization today is in a way, accomplishing her goal: Black Americans, making up about 12 percent of the population, account for over one-third of the nation's abortions.

Sanger's efforts to manage our population from the top is frightening mainly because it shows just how many in the radical left elite think. Give them some theoretical scheme to "save the world," and grant them the power to do so, and they will charge ahead full blast, with no second thoughts. And, since the goals often appear worthy, many well-meaning people will join in advocacy, without considering the consequences. Sanger warned us, in *The Pivot of Civilization,* that uncontrolled fertility is weakening the human race, increasing poverty, causing overcrowding, and allowing an increase in undesirable genetic traits.[84]

The scary part is that she was at least partially correct, and people like her will someday attempt to solve such problems in undesirable ways. There is a history of our smartest people, with the utmost confidence, pursuing paths that cause more harm than good. But the idea of perfecting the human capital of a country, rather than allowing the average quality to decline, makes sense from a purely logical point of view. The problem will be who's going to select the fittest, and what criteria will they use? Since Thomas Edison was a stupid and unruly student, and Stephen Hawkins had physical disabilities, would people like them be the first to go?

Charles Rubin has described a future dominated by the trans-humanist movement which calls for the biological "adjustment" of human beings into more perfect specimens. We read every day of advances in stem cell research, the transplantation of human organs, and the many pharmaceutical methods of individual enhancement. Those practices sound fine, but the trans-humanists take such medical marvels to the ultimate level. One such writer even suggests the eventual possibility of transferring a human brain into a robot! Such possible actions are touted as beneficial, but they are little different from Huxley's future where such medical practices are used to make people more pliable and docile. In any case, such a future would be the end of mankind as we know it. The constraints of Christian morality might prevent such modern "enlightened progress," but don't bet on it!

Sadly, our governing elites tend to think abstractly, along ideological lines that revere fine theories over common sense and established moral guidelines. For them, the theoretical end always justifies the messy means, so it is natural for them to employ big government's overwhelming powers to force feed their ideas about achieving a better world onto the ignorant people under their care. It is very possible that those who despair of controlling a nation's increasingly dependent and unruly subjects could eventually push an agenda similar to the scenario of Huxley's *Brave New World* or the trans-humanist adjustments where the elites have learned to manage the genetic and procreative processes of the masses to weed out the undesirables and make every one into a joyless but controllable automaton.

A democratic government that resorts to biological and chemical methods in order to maintain control over its people sounds preposterous. However, we already have schools that indoctrinate our children into accepting government regulation and a large degree of control over their lives. We have a growing class of people totally dependent on the government for their food, housing, medical care, and whatever else they can get. There is a growing drug culture with readily available substances to lull our minds. These developments are making many people both mentally and physically dependent on the government. It's the mental dependency that hurts most, the attitude of total helplessness that prevents meaningful action by a growing portion of the public. Any government action that advances such a spirit of submission and defeat in its people will undermine the very source of our nation's strength.

Our assistance programs have not just impaired potential contributions from the public but has also fueled a growing sense of entitlement. The intent, of course, was that these programs would make life easier for the claimants. But instead we see demands for more benefits, accompanied by riots, arson, and looting in civil disturbances by those individuals who have grievances and other self-perceived unmet needs. And the list of possible grievances has gotten so extensive that it includes such things as merely feeling "uncomfortable" or "offended" by another person's words or actions. Clearly, the times, and our culture, have changed since John Wooden was a kid and his father told him to never whine, complain or make excuses.

At some tipping point, with more and more people dependent on the government, and more demands and riots creating civil unrest, with the Washington leadership dead-locked over ideologies, the Chinese assuming world leadership, and the economy stagnating, perhaps sooner than one thinks, something will have to give. America's businesses can only advance productivity so far. And the minority still working can only bear so much.

When the final straw is added, and crunch time comes, there could be two kinds of riots—those people still working will demonstrate at having to support all those not working, and those not working will riot to demand more. We are drifting toward an impossible crisis. The authorities could be forced to declare martial law; then a reduction of subsidies for those who are disabled, unemployed, handicapped, and living in poverty; and finally, they might seek a "new and improved method" to neutralize the objections of its critics. A bio-chemical adjustment of newborns could render the citizenry so much more perfect and cooperative!

On a brighter note, before we slide into such a disastrous crisis, wouldn't we be well advised to try and save America? Sure, we have a huge and growing population, but that's just more reason to get it all under control and free of graft and corruption. A single minded president could do it. It's mostly a matter of just eliminating the obstacles that are holding us back: Cut out the deficit spending; break up the Wall Street banks; prosecute corruption with a zero tolerance policy; stop meddling in foreign intrigues and wars; de-centralize the government; re-emphasize states' rights; and appoint experienced people who have demonstrated superior management ability to run the government. No matter how tough that all might be, it pales in comparison to the alternative fate that we may be headed toward.

Chapter 21

GOOD MANAGEMENT
COULD TRUMP IDEOLOGY

A merica's two most recent elections were focused on "change" and "hope" but, after almost eight years we all must concede that, except for the very rich at the top, there has been little or no improvement for most Americans. Indeed, with the Federal Register getting more than sixty thousand pages of regulations added every year we do not need "change" as much as the competent administration of existing laws. If we could just find a way to eliminate the waste, inefficiency, and corruption that everyone knows poisons our federal government that would be change enough. In other words, if there were to be a beneficial "transformation" of our government it could come simply from competent management more than from ideological hopes and utopian dreams.

The confusion that cripples our government is caused by the ideological stalemate in Washington between the two political parties. They are locked in battle over hot ideological topics that have little to do with sound operations. While they argue, hundreds of unelected agencies are wielding power and issuing regulations helter-skelter that burden the nation's people and businesses. The fundamental problem is that ideological goals have taken precedence over sound management. Transforming America has taken precedence over running the government. But, remember this: America is fine, it's the government that needs work!

Professional politicians adore the divisive social issues that motivate voters to their side. The passions ignited by such topics as gun control are useful to distract attention from the poor performance of their representatives in Washington. Promising voters that they will manage the government intelligently is apparently just not sexy enough to distract from their sins or to garner enough votes and contributions to get re-elected!

This preoccupation with ideology is a relatively new phenomenon in American politics. Some of it is encouraged by politicians as a smoke screen but some comes from the apparently sincere passion of intellectuals. It is not a coincidence that, as our elites have lost their passion for religion, they have replaced it with a passion for abstract ideological programs. It is that passion over possible social changes that has come to dominate their energy, obliterating their interest in the simple but vitally important mechanics of running a country. If we are to restore American greatness, we must first ignore or lower the current fanaticism over the relatively unimportant issues and get back to the basic business of tending to the nuts and bolts that make us successful.

America has many intelligent and honest individuals who have extensive executive experience but few of them ever run for office. It seems that you almost have to be a liar and a crook to succeed at politics. You have to shake down all the big givers and corporations for donations just to finance an election. And to stay in office, you have to play ball with some bad bed fellows and make deals with cronies who support you. The good people that find a way into politics usually get eaten alive, and they either join the corrupt festivities or leave. The result has been the recent steady decline in our national fortune.

We lost the chance for reform during the last seven years because we picked a president who promised ideological solutions to strengthen gay rights, reduce income inequality, improve women's rights, create racial harmony, release the imprisoned terrorists, punish the wealthiest 1%, bring home our young men from the Middle East, and so forth. We can say with hindsight that none of those objectives were realized, and some got worse!

More importantly, during that wasted period, the government became bigger, more wasteful, the economy stagnated, the bankers from Wall Street were left in charge of the economy and grew much richer, and for half the people, the pursuit of happiness became a lost hope.

It is worth noting that the alternative candidate was a reasonably experienced executive who probably would have brought both integrity and good management to the Oval Office. But in that election, sadly, ideology trumped executive ability. It would be a form of insanity to repeat that historical mistake.

The situation is so bad, and so clearly the fault of both political parties, that Democratic Senator Jim Webb is wondering who to support for president. He points out that with Hillary Clinton we will just get more of the same thing. And he asks, "Do you want more of the same thing?" Clearly not. Webb considers Donald Trump to be a good alternative because he is "the only one who has the courage to step forward and say we've got to clean the stables of the government, we've got to make it work." Thus, a

Democratic senator is prepared to consider a Republican, because the other candidates just don't have the courage or determination to make the essential reforms. It all confirms the importance of a book's subtitle I have used: "Guts, Grit, and Common Sense."[85] A person's attitude, his or her grit, is so important in life that it can trump school grades, conservative or liberal principles, and debating skills.

In the past, democracies in trouble have eventually had to turn to a dictator to restore order. And sometimes that has worked well—not all despots are bad! One of the most celebrated modern despots turned Singapore from a backward outpost in Southeast Asia into an industrial and financial powerhouse and in so doing, gave his people enormous increases in prosperity. Like some old-fashioned fathers, he didn't hesitate to wield a whip when needed. His method of governance was expressed in no uncertain terms: to paraphrase, "If you want to live in a civilized society you must practice self discipline and restraint; however, if you do not want to behave we will make you."

Under Kuan Yew's firm guidance, Singapore became one of the safest places to visit in the world because the people behaved!

Singapore, like all Asian nations, had little or no experience with democracy. But after World War II, the attraction of open and free economies was seen by many as the secret weapon of the Western democracies. And, it had worked well in Hong Kong for a long time even under autocratic rule. So it made sense to adopt the free enterprise model of capitalism, but maintain a firm hand on the people who had no cultural familiarity with the responsibilities of democracy.

In America, we are well grounded in democracy and have no need to go that route, although many of our citizens do seem to have lost all familiarity with the responsibilities of democracy! But we do need to recognize a dysfunctional system when it becomes so obvious and make better choices in picking our leaders.

General Eisenhower-Won WWII and warned us about foreign military entanglements

Voters should also accept the fact that both democracies and republics are fragile systems. In addition to a free market they usually enjoy a culturally uniform population possessing similar religious and moral values. Those similarities make the people more cooperative and better team players than those found in societies fractured by race, religion, and competing principles. However, as they grow in size, developing huge populations, a diverse flood of immigrants, and competing views of the world, a democracy's unity crumbles. At the end of their days, democracies can look to only four possible futures: being overrun by conquerors, falling into a stagnant lethargy, allowing an autocrat to take control, or going back to basics and cleaning house. The last possibility is clearly the best, and requires minimizing ideological squabbles and concentrating on restoring fairness, honesty, and sound management to national affairs. All that's needed is a strong, rational, and seasoned executive who has demonstrated such qualities from real-world experience.

In sharp contrast to our government's inability to function effectively, either here or abroad, many huge American multinational businesses operate successfully throughout the world. Many have manufacturing and distribution facilities in more than one hundred countries and get along amicably with the host nation's people and their governments. Their executives have been trained and seasoned to lead the company decisively. Before they get to leadership positions, they've had to work their way up in the business for decades and display the required results that justify giving them the power to lead. That corporate management obviously works well but America turns over its leadership and management to a new rookie every four years, and usually to one with virtually no administrative experience. No wonder the government is snafued!

In short, our giant corporate businesses are run rationally by experienced administrators, and most of them, given similar authority, would do better managing the country than our recent presidents. Imagine someone going in and appointing competent people to run all the agencies, instead of all the political hacks that are currently appointed and who sit as figureheads over every branch of the government. Imagine a professional manager straightening out the computer systems that today cannot keep track of visitors overstaying their visa dates and the few hundred thousand names on the no-fly list; not to mention a president who would make sure that the millions of people over 100 years old were taken off the social security lists! All that could happen. Those things need doing. Most of our corporate presidents do that kind of stuff all the time. Why can't we elect an American president who can do the same? It's not rocket science!

Chapter 22

WAS HUXLEY RIGHT?

Aldous Huxley wrote many books, and gave many lectures, but his most lasting contribution was his depressing predictions of our future. They serve as a wake-up call that illustrates what could happen if we do not restore the primacy of liberty over dependency. If we allow a dependent class, deficient in self-reliance and initiative, to grow inexorably, there could be little choice other than Huxley's grim scenario. And the problem, he suggests, isn't what Malthus warned of—a shortage of adequate food and material goods.

Huxley believed that the biggest threat to democracies was the rapid and continuing growth in a nation's population, which of necessity seems to require increased supervision, organization, and regulation—the enemies of individual liberty. He made the case that these pressures would destroy democracies, and it seems more and more possible that he was right!

Huxley projected a future world where the leaders had abandoned the current cumbersome methods of controlling their subjects with media spin, secret deals, news blitzes, indoctrination in school, and rigged elections. Instead, they resorted to genetic control, applying drugs to embryos that rendered them malleable and simple, like the drones in an ant hill or the worker bees following their instinctive coding in the queen bee's service. Huxley's dystopian views were inspired, not by the problems of finances, food supply, or social issues, but by recognizing the difficult and ornery nature of most people. In his book, he describes a time when there were just too many people, and they could never agree on anything. What else could the leaders do? Science had the answer, religion had become irrelevant, and by neutralizing all opposition the elected elite could make the world a more perfect place!

Such a future scenario is out there, and it's scary if you stop for a moment to consider what might happen. If you worry about what kind of life your grandchildren will have, and are concerned about the future of the country, that's good; but, you are probably worrying about the wrong things. Your concerns are probably focused on the so-called "problems" our nation faces, the ones the news media warn about: the costs and constant meddling of big government; the ballooning national debt; global warming; the endless battles over gay rights and abortion; race riots, looting and burning in our major cities; illegal immigration; the failure of schools, and so on. Granted, these types of issues need to be solved, but why is it so difficult?

Perhaps all our nation's failings are just symptoms of a deeper malaise? Could our sickness be simply because we elect incompetent people—people with little or no experience in sound management skills? Myron Caplan has told us why many voters will make bad decisions if those decisions make them feel good about themselves.[86] But, for Pete's sake, how can this mess we have created in Washington make people feel good, even if their candidate promises to make things better? The promises get better and better during each election cycle, but, face it—the nation just keeps getting in worse shape after each election. As they say, if the promises sound too good to be true, they probably are lies.

> **On Excessive Compassion:**
>
> "The lessons of history... show conclusively that continued dependence upon relief induces a spiritual and moral disintegration fundamentally destructive to the national fibre."
>
> President Franklin D. Roosevelt

The problem areas described above make up much of the news, but when you boil it all down, the real question is: What kind of people will share my grandchildren's life? What kind of people will inhabit the country? How will those men and women be different from us? Will their attitudes, personal traits, and goals be different from ours? Will a corrupt government handing out welfare make cheaters out of the people? Will sharia law replace ours? And, mostly, do we want our grandchildren to live in that world of the future? If not, we can and should do whatever possible to shape that future; to make a better place for future generations to live in. Always remember that cultures are what we make them, and we have some serious re-shaping to do!

It is self-evident that the nation's problems, and its strengths, come from its people. Governments are simply the systems established by people to regulate their day to day affairs and protect themselves from invasion. And we can design any type of government we want. Just as you design your house, or its yard, you can arrange your government in the way best to suit your needs and wants. Broadly speaking, either, (1) you create a culture that allows everyone a certain amount of freedom in return for their assuming a certain amount of personal responsibility, or (2) you arrange for the government to solve most of your problems and cater to your needs, and in return, give up most of your liberty to do and live as you wish. There will be some income inequality in the first case, but in the second case, reducing income inequality and enjoying liberty will be completely beyond your control!

We have argued in this book that the care and feeding of human beings is a soft-science, subject to chaos theory, so full of variables and uncertainties that nothing about their actions can be predicted. However, in the operation of governments there are a few general rules, and five of them are these:

1.) Poverty and need will always increase in direct proportion to the money made available for their relief. Applicants for aid are basically normal human beings and they will find ways to take advantage and get as much as they can.

2.) Every new demand to get something from the government increases one's dependence on the government and reduces the recipient's personal liberty. Once you ask for food stamps they will tell you what you can spend it on. Once you demand medical care, they can tell you how much you can have, when you can have it, and when they will pull the plug. If you ask for housing they will tell you where to live. If you rely on public schools they will dictate what is taught to your children. And so on and on it

goes. Everything given by government is a trade-off;
the recipient loses certain rights.

3.) If you subsidize people having babies they will have
more babies. If those parents aren't able to take care
of themselves, they probably won't be able to take
care of their children, and how will those children
learn how to care for theirs?

4.) Rewarding bad behavior is just as harmful for
humans as it is for pets. A government that encourages dependency will end up with lap dogs instead
of responsible adults.

5.) Many nations have grown and prospered, expanded
borders, and conquered new lands-until overextended and bankrupted by the costs. Debilitating
foreign entanglements are one of the recurring
nightmares of nations.

On a national level, when a major block of the citizenry
have given up their rights in return for the security of an
all-mothering government, the burden falls on the self-supporting people. They are faced with the cost of taking care
of those dependent on the government. The top economic
class doesn't care as long as they can keep ripping off their
lion's share of the economy. Those at the bottom don't care
as long as the checks keep coming. It's the working class in
the middle that carries the load for both groups, but that

long suffering group cannot support everyone else for long. Everything they can make is stolen by those on the top and most of what's left is taken by the government and given to those at the bottom. If we are to save America there has to be a restoration of fairness. We cannot continue rewarding bad behavior and punishing good behavior.

In modern democracies like America, the law of survival of the fittest has been reversed. Today, the competitive struggle has become a matter of who can find the best way to support him or herself in an advanced and complex society. For many people, getting on the government gravy-train has become an attractive option. The alternative, working and paying taxes, could result in a lower after-tax income. Plus, if you opt for the welfare route, you can work part-time, get additional tax-free income, and have more leisure time. Unless you have fairly bright employment opportunities, the choice becomes a no-brainer. That is how America's tax and welfare policies have worked to undermine both the married nuclear family and the incentive to work at less than high paying jobs. And it is self-perpetuating—the more people who choose the unmarried welfare path, the more seductive that alternative becomes for the suckers still working. That is why Ben Franklin knew, hundreds of years ago, that the safety net should not offer recipients the same level of affluence and self-respect as that enjoyed by the working class. It's just a matter of fairness; and accepting the laws of human motivation.

The record of the last few decades has revealed that the number of people getting assistance keeps growing. The number supporting them is getting smaller. The least fit, who get the assistance, will eventually suffocate the nation, because they are reproducing at a faster rate than the families supporting them.

> "Extremism in the defense of liberty is no vice. And moderation in the pursuit of justice is no virtue."
>
> ---Barry Goldwater

The real problem underlying this welfare issue is money. America could provide unlimited welfare forever if we could afford it. If we had a balanced budget, our finances could support largesse. The programs might still undermine the nature of our citizenry, but we would at least be solvent. Thus, welfare systems need not be ideologically driven. There are two rational guidelines to direct us, derived simply from sound management principles: (1) Total government expenditures, including welfare, should be limited to total government income. (2) Assistance payments should increase the recipient's after tax income to something less than that of working people. Welfare must be recognized as a charitable safety-net, not an alternative way of life.

If no change is made, America's huge deficits and growing debts will eventually bankrupt us. Future presidents will have to deal with the growing number of dependent and demanding citizens by rationing what they get but then the supplicants will riot. With civil anarchy, the solution could go either the way Orwell described, or the way Huxley described. The only way to avoid such desperate scenarios is to seek policies that will reverse the downward course we are on. Excessive compassion will lead to bankruptcy. Ideological battles will create divisive groups and stalemate. Democracy has a weak underbelly. It requires an honest hard-working people at the bottom, and competent managers in the nations' capitols. It will take the straight-talking firmness of a non-ideological leader to overcome our downward course. It will take a lot of tough love, but now may be the time to get tough.[87]

The difficult choices described above illustrate the importance of maintaining the best qualities of a people. It's not a matter of whether the next generation will be Republicans or Democrats, liberal or conservative, religious or agnostic, and not about their mere appearance, fat or thin, or tall or short. I mean what will make them tick: Will they be more or less competent than us? Will they support the American culture, be more or less honest, be more or less brave, or be innovative or lazy? I'm talking about that kind of thing: the qualities that determine what they do, how they do it, and whether the nation they live in will prosper and allow the full pursuit of their happiness. For a nation is no more than the sum of its people. Great people and great cultures make great nations; inferior people and inferior cultures make inferior nations.

The corruption, the bad schools, the deficit—they all can be taken care of IF the people care about them and actually do something about them. Right now, no one's doing anything except arguing! And very few face the facts or speak the truth! Telling the truth requires less tact and a dose of bluntness; it can be unpleasant, but the ugly truth is better than the deceit of papering over the lies fed to us by our current gang of leaders.

If you are impassioned over such hot topics as Camp Gitmo, gun control, and climate change, you may, like many voters, be unmoved by the almost universal mismanagement and corruption in government. But everyone knows that our failed in management prevents rational discussion of all the other issues. Entitlement reform is primarily a matter of simple management of available resources to provide assistance to the truly needy. Ideology gets in the way of turning these public programs into fair and reasonable support systems. In the same vein, we cannot continue to meddle in foreign affairs on someone else's dime. America, rich as she is, does not have unlimited money to spend. Until we recognize that fact, we are like the family which continues to put off the unpleasantness of a budget, yet knows it needs doing, hates to start, but is continually worried by the knowledge that it must be done.

Every generation brings a whole new crop of people inhabiting the earth. They may look similar to prior generations, but they are different inside. Populations do change. Whether you are an American, or a citizen of any other national or ethnic group, the nature of your people will be different in fifty years, just as we are different from those of fifty years ago. For these purposes the past doesn't matter, and human origins are irrelevant. You may believe in the intelligent design of mankind, or divine creation, the Garden of Eden, or Darwin's descent of man from the primates, or even some type of alien invasion or interference. But, none of that matters for the future, because the future is in our hands, and what we make of it matters.

President John F. Kennedy told us years ago to "Ask not what the country can do for you, but what you can do for the country." Very few paid attention to his words. Many ignored them and demanded more from the government. Now, fifty years later, let's honor "Jack's" memory by doing something on our own—Be wary of anyone who tells you all the things he or she will have the government do for you. It's time for *you* to do something for the country! Support leaders outside the corrupt political class. Encourage those candidates who have shown they are tough enough and honest enough to do what has been needed for a long time. It is time we take action, clean house, and make America the exceptional country she was destined to be.

NOTES

1. George Phillies, *Peace Now-Eisenhower Was Right*, (The Standard Times editorial, New Bedford MA, February 8, 2016)

2. Ibid, George Phillies...

3. Ben Carson, *America the Beautiful* (Grand Rapids: Zondervan, 2012), 195

4. Thomas Sowell, *A Conflict of Visions, Ideological Origins of Political Struggles* (New York: Basic Books, 2002)

5. Theodore Dalrymple, *Life at the Bottom, The Worldview That Makes the Underclass* (New York: Ivan R. Dee), 2003

6. John Wooden and Steve Jamison, *The Essential Wooden* (New York, Mc Graw-Hill, 2007)

7. Edward Lorenz, *The Essence of Chaos Theory* (Washington: The University of Washington Press, 1995)

8. Thomas J. Stanley, *The Millionnaire Mind* (Kansas City:Andrews Mc Meel Publishing, L.L.C., 2001)

9. Colin Renfrew, *Prehistory*: *The Making of the Modern Mind* (New York: The Modern Library, 2008), p92

10. Renfrew, Ibid, p109

11. Renfrew, Ibid, p78

12. Renfrew, Ibid, p79

13. Daniel Coyle, *The Talent Code; Greatness Isn't Born, It's Grown* (New York, Bantam Books, 2009)

14. Robert Epstein, *The Case Against Adolescence* (Sanger CA: Quill Driver Books, 2007) 4-5

15. Ludwig Von Mises, *Human Action* (Irvington-on-Hudson: The Foundation for Economic Education, Inc., 1949) 650-652

16. Robert H. Frank, *Passions Within Reason, The Strategic Role of the Emotions* (New York: W. W. Norton & Company, 1988), 253

17. Carmen Bin Laden, *Inside the Kingdom* (New York: Warner Books, 2004)199-201

18. Michael S. Gazzaniga, *Who's in Charge? Free Will and the Science of the Brain* (Harper Collins, 40 Anniversary, The Gifford Lectures, 2011)

19. Ibid, 127

20. ©2006 Steve Connor, News.independent.co.uk/world/ science_technology/article, 11/23/3006

21. Victor Davis Hanson, *The Other Greeks* (Berkeley: University of California Press, 1999) 99-101

22. Gregory Clark, *A Farewell to Alms-A Brief Economic History of the World* (*Princeton*: Princeton University Press, 2007), 268-71

23. Gregory Clark, Interviewed by Kevin Drum for *Mother Jones*, February 5, 2014

24. Thomas B. Carson, *Beyond the American dream; Work and Wealth in the 21st Century* (Bloomington: First Books Library. 1998), 10

25. Thomas F. Madden, *Venice, A New History* (New York: Penguin Books, 2012), 9

26. Madden, Ibid., 9-10

27. Madden, Ibid., 29

28. Madden, Ibid., 29

29. Dan Senor and Shimon Peres, *Start-Up Nation, The Story Of Israel's Economic Miracle* (New York: Twelve, Hachette Book Group, 2009), 222

30. Barbara Tuchman, *The First Salute* (New York: Alfred A. Knopf, 1988), 89-90

31. George Will, *With a Happy Eye, But* . . . (New York: The Free Press, 2002) 20.

32. Dan Senor, op cit.

33. Huff Post-World, March 5, 2015, First They Come for the Women...

34. Robert Conquest, *Reflections on a Ravaged Century* (New York: W. W. Norton & Company, 2000)

35. Philip Short, *Pol Pot: The Anatomy of a Nightmare* (New York: Henry Holt and Company, 2004)

36. Robert Conquest, op. cit.

37. Arthur Koestler, *Darkness at Noon* (New York: Bantam Books, 1968), 209-211)

38. David Horowitz, *Unholy Alliance, Radical Islam and the American Left* (Washington, DC: Regnery Publishing, Inc., 2004), 66-67

39. Charles T. Rubin, *The Eclipse of Man* (New York: Encounter Books, 2014), 168

40. Tamin Ansary, *Destiny Disrupted, A History of the World Through Islamic Eyes* (New York: Public Affairs Books, 2009), 110-115 and 270-272

41. George F. Thomas, *Christian Ethics and Moral Philosophy* (New York: Charles Scribner's Sons, 1955) 434

42. Thomas Cahill, *How The Irish Saved Civilization* (New York: Anchor Books Doubleday, 1995), 140-42

43. Arthur Herman, *How the Scots Invented the Modern World* (New York: Three Rivers Press, 2001), 15

44. Richard P. Feynman, *The Meaning of It All; Thoughts of a Citizen Scientist* (Reading MA: Helix Books/ Addison Wesley, 1998), 115

45. Edoardo Albert, *Ibn Sina, A Concise Life* (Markfield UK: Kube Publishing, 2013), 37

46. Arthur Koestler, op. cit.

47. P. T. Bauer, *Reality and Rhetoric; Studies in the Economics of Development* (Boston: Harvard University Press, 1984), 5

48. Bill Greene, *Common Genius*, (Little Rock: Laissez Faire Books, 2007), 13

49. James A. Michener, *Poland* (New York: Dial Press, 2015)

50. S. J. Taylor, *Stalin's Apologist: Walter Duranty: the Nrw York Times Man in Moscow* (Oxford UK: The Oxford University Press, 1990)

51. http://www.nationsreportcard.gov

52. John Kao, *Innovation Nation* (New York: Free Press, 2007)

53. Ben Stein and Phil DeMuth, *Can America Survive?* (Carlsbad CA: Hay House, New Beginning Press, 2004), xxix

54. *The Daily Signal*, February 8, 2016

55. Robert Rector and Rachel Sheffield, *Maine Food Stamp Work Requirement Cuts Non-Parent Caseload by 80 Percent* (Heritage Foundation on line Backgrounder # 3091)

56. Newsmax, February 15, 2016 News at Newsmax. com http://www.newsmax.com/US/ssa-audit-millions- dead/2015/03/10/id/629253/#ixzz40Fxi3jjl

57. Michael D. Tanner, an article in the Los Angeles Times-Online, August 22, 2013.

58. Tanner, op. cit.

59. Tanner, op. cit.

60. Bryan Caplan, *The Myth of the Rational Voter; Why Democracies Choose Bad Policies* (Princeton: Princeton University Press, 2007)

61. Scott Adams, *How to Fail at Almost Everything and Still Win Big* (Penguin Portfolio, 2013), 117

62. Peter D. Salins, *The Smart Society; Strengthening America's Greatest Resource, Its People* (New York: Encounter Books, 2014), 215

63. Salins, ibid 2

64. Salins, Ibid 3

65. Salins, Ibid 5

66. Salins, Ibid 64

67. Michael S. Gazzaniga, *Nature's Mind, The Biological Roots of Thinking, Emotions, Sexuality, Language, and Intelligence* (New York: Basic Books, 1992),186

68. Julian L. Simon, *The Ultimate Resource* (Princeton NJ: The Princeton University Press, 1981), 41

69. Robert H. Frank, *The Darwin Economy* (Princeton: Princeton University Press, 2001), 84-85

70. Robert H. Frank, op. cit., 251

71. Peter Salins, op. cit. 13-14

72. Roger J. Williams, *The Human Frontier* (New York: Harcourt, Brace and Company, 1946), 156

73. Daniel Goleman, *Emotional Intelligence* (New York: Bantam Books, 2006)

74. Robert Sternberg, *Wisdom, Intelligence, and Creativity Synthesized* (Cambridge, UK: Cambridge University Press, 2007)

75. Howard Gardner, *Frames of Mind, The Theory of Multiple Intelligences* (New York: Basic Books, 1923

76. Thomas J. Stanley and William D. Danko, *The Millionaire Next Door* (Adams GA: Longstreet press, 1996)

77. Roger J. Williams, *Free & Unequal; The Biological Basis of Liberty* (Indianapolis: Liberty Press, 1953), 127

78. Ibid, 129

79. James R. Flynn, *What is Intelligence?* (Cambridge, UK: Cambridge University Press, 2009)

80. Bill Greene, *Wasted Genius; How IQ and SAT Tests Are Hurting Our Kids and Crippling America* (Lancaster NH: Lost Nation Books, 2011)

81. Statista, *The Statistical Portal*

82. Richard Fenigsen, *Other People's Lives: Reflections on Medicine, Ethics, and Euthanasia* (Terra Haute: Issues in Law & Medicine, Vol. 28, No.2, Fall 2012), 266

83. Fenigsen, op. cit., 95-96

84. Margaret Sanger, *The Pivot of Civilization* (London: Jonathan Cape, 1923)

85. Bill Greene, Common Genius, op. cit.

86. Caplan, op. cit.

87. Donald J. Trump, *It's Time to Get Tough* (Washington DC: Regnery Publishing, 2011)

ABOUT THE AUTHOR

B ill Greene has been engaged in the management of organizations and a variety of businesses since earning his MBA from Babson College and working at the Harvard Graduate  School of Business Administration. He is the author of Common Genius, Wasted Genius, and several books on business administration, economic history, and the art of rearing children and improving school systems.

Educated at Princeton, Babson, and Harvard, Greene remains active in politics, schooling, and the study of economics and history. He and his wife, Cathy, have nine children and sixteen grandchildren; and live in New England with two dogs, ten chickens, and a herd of Hereford cattle.